The Nation's Favourite Churches

The
Nation's
Favourite
Churches

Andrew Barr

LION

Copyright © 2006 Andrew Barr
This edition copyright © 2006 Lion Hudson

The author asserts the moral right to be
identified as the author of this work

A Lion Book
an imprint of
Lion Hudson plc
Mayfield House, 256 Banbury Road,
Oxford OX2 7DH, England
www.lionhudson.com

ISBN 13: 978 0 7459 5220 8
ISBN 10: 0 7459 5220 8

First edition 2006
10 9 8 7 6 5 4 3 2 1 0

By arrangement with the BBC
BBC logo © BBC 1996
Songs of Praise logo © BBC 2000

The BBC logo and Songs of Praise logo are registered
trademarks of the British Broadcasting Corporation
and are used under licence.

A catalogue record for this book is available
from the British Library

Printed and bound in China

For my family, the Sheehans in Australia
and the Bradfords in New Zealand, who
gave me space and peace in their homes
to write this book

Contents

Foreword

As a child the words 'church' and 'favourite' were not a natural combination for me. Since that childhood aversion, however, churches have played an increasingly important role in my life. Looking back now, I can see that my life has been measured – or at least marked – by an increasing number of churches. I cannot identify the actual moment of my growing interest, but today my three sons are quick to mock my enthusiasm for a 'quick' look around each and every church we pass. I admit to being an unashamed church enthusiast and never miss a chance to visit both ancient and modern places of worship whenever I can.

Sometimes it is a chance to join with others in worship, and to sing songs of praise, but at other times it is an opportunity to be alone with my thoughts. Churches of whatever size and shape have that ability to transport one to another place, a sacred space infused with the prayers of generations. It's a place where one is never really alone and a space where prayer and praise come easily.

Of course, as the editor of *Songs of Praise*, I have been given both the opportunity and the excuse to visit many churches and congregations up and down the country as well as abroad. They all have different associations for me and I now have a significant number of favourite churches.

I am grateful to Andrew for both a reminder of past locations and for a number of suggestions of possible venues for the future. Memories of St Paul's Cathedral following the death of Princess Diana and Westminster Abbey following the 9/11 bombings are particularly poignant and act as vivid reminders of the times that *Songs of Praise* provided a focus for public grief. But alongside those are recollections of cream teas from Ottery St Mary and smoked haddock in the shadow of Oban Cathedral. Such is the power of churches to mark both the important and the ordinary within life and the reason why each one holds special significance for both individuals and communities.

In this treasury of locations, Andrew has succeeded in cataloguing not only a rich mix of church buildings but also an even richer number of reasons for their popularity. As always he mixes history, music, theology and personal anecdotes together in a way that brings bricks and mortar to life. I found it inspiring and challenging.

Hugh Faupel

Editor
Songs of Praise

Introduction

This is the story of a journey around Britain to visit and explore thirty buildings that have become much-loved landmarks. More importantly, it is where the story of each community who live around them is being lived out and its own distinctive Christian faith newly experienced and created by each succeeding generation.

The Nation's Favourite Churches is a story of places and people.

'You've set yourself an impossible task,' said one of the presenters of a BBC local radio station, interviewing me on a summer Sunday morning as preparations for the journey began. 'Do you really think that you can name everyone's favourite church? Surely there are enough to fill dozens of books!'

Certainly, the task would have been impossible even to begin were it not for the audiences who listen each week to the Sunday breakfast shows from their local radio stations; many of the churches featured on this journey were nominated by these listeners and helped lay out our itinerary. Some of the nation's favourite churches that I visited on my journey are grand places, landmarks famous around the world, while others are small, hidden away and almost unknown, yet as devotedly loved by handfuls of dedicated people. Between them they have given me a picture of the wide sweep of church life within Britain today. Some of these churches will have featured on *Songs of Praise* over its forty-five-year history with a few being so popular that they have provided the setting for the programme on more than one occasion. Others, however, are patiently waiting their turn and hoping that one day they will also be able to share their story with the many millions of viewers who make a regular Sunday evening date with *Songs of Praise*.

The writer and politician, Roy Hattersley, said that the English landscape is only complete when a church built within fifty years of the Norman Conquest is visible, like the church of St Mary the Virgin at the centre of the hilltop village of Goudhurst in the Kentish High Weald. This church takes its place in the thirty featured on the journey not only because it was the setting for a particularly inspiring episode of *Songs of Praise* but also because it helped give me an idea of how to make this book different from some of the many fine guides that have appeared over the centuries since William Camden's *Britannia* or Daniel Defoe's *Tour through the Whole Island of Great Britain*.

For ten years, 'church' for me was this ancient building in Goudhurst, founded in 1170 by Robert de Crevecour, a Norman knight. More than 800 years later, I was the stranger the congregation made welcome. In doing so, I learned why so many people come back time and again from all over the world to visit this church at the top of the village high street, discovering what happens when you have both the time and opportunity to get to know a building, its people and their stories. This book tries to describe the nation's favourite churches through the eyes of the people who love them.

One Sunday morning during the reading of the Banns of Marriage, a truly unexciting part of a church service unless you happen to be the betrothed, I was daydreaming when a trick of the light made me look again at the wall of the nave at some marks which I must have looked at many times before. I realized for the first time that they showed where the pulpit had been fixed, nearly 250 years

Daniel Defoe, 1660–1731

before, during the English Civil War. This long-vanished feature, tidied away by a Victorian benefactor in 1860, was not only where the congregation had heard over many centuries the formal notice of weddings and been given the opportunity to raise objections, but also from where at gunpoint one of Oliver Cromwell's soldiers had removed James Wilcocke, the vicar in the days when Royalist supporters of King Charles I were fighting Parliamentarians.

Len, a twentieth-century member of the choir and still singing with them well into his nineties, vividly transported me back to the fateful year 1640. He told me that his account would be found in no guidebook, but instead had been handed down by word of mouth over many generations. Waving his walking stick as if it were a blunderbuss, he dropped his customary mellifluous tone to become a Roundhead officer as he exclaimed, 'Sir, who stand preaching up there: come down or I'll shoot you down!'

Apparently Mr Wilcocke had done his bidding. Len said that this incident was much welcomed by the congregation, who had found their preacher to be 'a man unfit, idle and frivolous'. They had already protested at the disappearance of their former vicar, 'a well-deserving minister, faithful and painful in preaching', removed from the parish 'but for what cause we know not'.

Songs of Praise viewers know that each programme can only scratch the surface of stories about the places visited. In the journey described in this book, there are many encounters, some extraordinary and a few even mysterious. I am very grateful to the many people who have found time to answer this visiting stranger's questions. Most were chance encounters, and what I heard revealed to me that the churches of Britain are far from being on their last legs.

In his guide of 1724, Daniel Defoe claims that the author will 'describe in his own fashion what is going on around him'. I have tried to do the same. I have had other literary companions on the way. John Betjeman's guide to *English Parish Churches*, which the late Poet-Laureate and fellow church-lover marked out for me, has set an agenda that will keep me travelling until the day of judgment. Then there is a slim volume published in 1847 by the Revd John Mason Neale, best known for his carol and hymn-writing. *A Church Tour through England and Wales* is a wonderful commentary on favourite churches seen through the eyes of a Victorian churchman, and includes some hilarious and caustic descriptions of the church in those days. Like both Betjeman and Neale, I have included a glossary of some of the terms that both architects and clergy use.

Daniel Defoe was very particular about correcting previously published accounts of churches by authors that he discovered had not actually been there. In his delight in visiting towers and steeples, he was outraged to discover when they did not always exist and that his journey had been in vain, as at Doncaster and York. Neale honourably marks in his index those churches which he had actually visited as distinct from others in which he

merely seems to have formed an impression. In my own long and fascinating journey around Britain, I have visited all the churches featured here, but just as Daniel Defoe wrote in his own introduction, will add that 'any mistake that can be found, and in a friendly manner hinted, we shall receive with thankfulness, and amend cheerfully'.

My thanks once again are due to Hugh Faupel, Editor of *Songs of Praise* at BBC Religion in Manchester, for his support; to Morag Reeve, Jono Self and Kate Leech at Lion Hudson for their advice, editorial input and making sense of the hundreds of photographs taken on the journey and to Simon Emery and Jonathan Roberts for their design work. My gratitude above all to Liz, whose knowledge of past programmes and wifely company on some of the journey, together with her own acute editorial eye, has made all the difference.

I never miss the opportunity to have a look in a church; it is an addiction that does no harm to someone who has spent so much of his life producing *Songs of Praise*. On the precise day that this foreword was written, I made my first visit to a church in New Zealand. Christ Church, Russell, in the North Island, is the country's oldest church but only celebrated its 170th birthday in 2006. Far away across the world from the churches of the Norman Conquest, in the country where the first ever *Songs of Praise* from the Commonwealth was made in 1970, the season of Advent was underway – and yet the fig tree was in leaf and oranges were ripe in the garden. There would be no bleak midwinter here at Christmas. I felt very far from home, but there was also much that was familiar in the service in this church which, like St Mary's, Goudhurst, is a part of the worldwide Anglican Communion. Listening to the choir singing words written by a distinguished local composer, I realized how every church, its building and its story, will always be somebody's favourite.

Andrew Barr

'Out of such sun and air
What Christ may come,
Shining with new and lovely light
On our dim and shrouded lives;
Stirring our sleepiness with dreams
Visions of life beyond compare,
Out of this sun and air
Come, Christ, however you will come.'

'Northland' by Colin Gibson

1

LONDON

The Royal Parish Church

*'**S**t Martin-in-the-Fields exists to honour God, and to enable questioning, open-minded people to discover for themselves the significance of Jesus Christ.'*

Mission statement of St Martin's

The journey begins at a church in the heart of the capital, at Charing Cross, the point from which the distance from London to everywhere else in the world is measured. One Monday morning late in 1922, a young Scotsman started a new job in an office on the Strand. He was to become the first director-general of the BBC, creating radio services which to this day are the envy of the world. John Reith wrote on that first day that he hadn't 'the faintest idea' what he was expected to do. His father was a Presbyterian minister, and this son of the manse thought that religion should be broadcast because 'the King was a Christian'.

But who was to come to the microphone?

By a most fortunate coincidence, the person who was to become one of the all-time greats of religious broadcasting was found just along the street from the new studio. He was the vicar of St Martin-in-the-Fields.

Dick Sheppard became vicar here in 1914, and throughout the First World War had opened the church daily to men who came in to pray before they were hurried across the road to Charing Cross station to catch the troop train to France. The few who survived the battles in the trenches would return to sit exhausted and shocked in the church. And like the widows and friends of those who did not return, they found solace in the preaching of a humane parson who understood what they had been through, and yet could retain belief in God.

Sheppard was to begin the art of communicating God's love to a new congregation: the unseen listener at home. As the BBC's programmes reached more and more people in Britain and then abroad, the names of St Martin-in-the-Fields and Dick Sheppard became synonymous with religious broadcasting.

Since that January evening in 1924, when Dick Sheppard stood in the church's spectacularly high pulpit for the very first outside-broadcast of a church service, BBC microphones have been present on literally hundreds of occasions and more recently, *Songs of Praise* television cameras too. A few broadcasts have coincided with tragic events such as the terrorist attack by suicide-bombers on London commuters in July 2005, and it has been the clergy and congregation of St Martin's who have responded, when the rest of us were lost for words.

Unfortunately, only a few fragments of Dick Sheppard's broadcast sermons can now be read, let alone heard, but some words from his friend and contemporary, Archbishop William Temple, have the same quality of 'good talk' which the founding father of the BBC, John Reith, was looking for and found in the vicar of St Martin's. William Temple went on the air in 1940, as invading armies once again threatened the freedom of the world.

H.R.L. (Dick) Sheppard 1880–1937; vicar of St Martin-in-the-Fields 1914–1926

'What light then do the cross and the resurrection throw upon the darkness of this present time? At best it can only be a broken and partial light that our human eyes can see. But there is light; light sufficient for us in the dark to rise by.'

The Parish Church of St Martin-in-the-Fields, London

In 1726, a new church was completed in the narrow streets of a fashionable area of London, west of Covent Garden market. Designed by a Scottish architect, James Gibbs, it was built on the foundations of an earlier church provided so that diseased corpses could be kept away from King Henry VIII's Royal Palace in Whitehall. In fact, so many corpses continued to be buried around and under the new church, that by 1774, the churchwardens were forced to put up this notice: 'No graves to be dug in any of the vaults as a practice which will in time endanger the foundations of the said church.'

It was a century later before the wide-open space of Trafalgar Square was formed and the famous view of the front of St Martin's appeared. Gibbs had 'perched' the steeple on the portico with the intention that the Christian spire would stand triumphant on Corinthian columns belonging to a pagan age. The pediment bears the royal arms of George I. This style was to be much copied in Scotland, Ireland and America, but has not met with universal approval, Nikolaus Pevsner describing it as 'a doubtful blessing'.

The spacious galleried interior is lit by two ranges of windows, and the ceiling is in the form of a barrel vault supported by more Corinthian columns. The plastered cherubs were made by two Italian masters of the art, Giovanni Bagutti and Guiseppe Arturi. The pews did not arrive until 1799, and the present organ, a Walker with 3,637 pipes, was built in 1990.

It is hard to realize that this famous building overlooking Trafalgar Square, visited each year by 700,000 tourists from all over the world, is also a parish church. It does, however, have some unusual duties, such as ringing its church bells to announce a naval victory. This is because the Admiralty – the headquarters of the Royal Navy – is in the parish. And although King George I was the first churchwarden of St Martin's, he carried exactly the same responsibilities and duties to the parish that I had in a small country church more than 250 years later.

What is the place of a parish church in the third millennium AD? This is the question that the present vicar of St Martin's, the Revd Nicholas Holtam, asks, as planning gets underway to give his church a new lease of life. It has involved creating public spaces under the church to replace the crypt, which in 1850 was condemned as unsuitable even for the burial of the dead of the parish.

'Man should pray in a room with windows'; this saying from the Talmud, reminding believers to remember their neighbours, is fully realized in a building whose doors are always open, and where someone will always be saying their prayers. Neighbours are not merely perceived and prayed for through St Martin's somewhat opaque windows; their needs are visible daily, in the crumpled figures of the homeless who come in and fall asleep in the pews. On occasion, a live BBC broadcast has even been accompanied by the sound of peaceful snoring. For this royal parish church, dedicated to the saint who divided his own cloak to give half to a beggar, is the church of the homeless, and has a special relationship with those who live rough on the streets.

The formal name given to this relationship is The Connection at St Martin's, a homeless centre. A former vicar of St Martin's, Austen Williams, said that when someone came to the door, they did not only want to be greeted with a sandwich, but also to be recognized as someone with a name, and to be remembered. And yet The Connection is not only about the persistent needs

'In The Beginning' by Mike Chapman, sculpted for St Martin's in 2000

of the poor. Nicholas Holtam says, 'If The Connection is about the transformation of lives of people who are homeless, the congregation is about the transformation of lives of people who "know their need of God". The mix of people here is electrifying.'

I learned a lot about this when I was a member of the adjoining parish of St James's, Piccadilly. During a particularly grim winter, the homeless overflowed into our building, and in just a few days many of those who had at first needed help had themselves become helpers. Perhaps that was why Lily-Ann decided to give time and energy to the organization of St James's when it was in the doldrums. Living on the streets, she used to arrive at PCC meetings with all her worldly possessions contained in two plastic bags. Although she couldn't wash regularly, ensuring that we had to keep the windows open whenever we met, it was often Lily-Ann that would come up with a new idea when the rest of us were flagging, especially ideas about raising money for the church. We needed her. She needed us.

This is what the vicar of St Martin's calls *Ubuntu* – a South African word meaning 'humanity towards others' or 'sharing, participating and belonging'. When we ask someone 'are you well?', the answer should be 'I am well if you are well'.

Nicholas Holtam worries that churches can be frustrating places, 'because they promise too much'. But at least this first church on our journey around the nation's favourites keeps its promises – continuing to provide the setting and inspiration for broadcasting all over the world, a home for the homeless and a welcoming community for people of many nations. A new Christmas crib for St Martin's had been made by Tomoaki Suzuki, a Japanese wood carver, who, having heard the story of the nativity for the first time from the vicar, chose to model his figures on the people of St Martin's and the surrounding community of the Square.

'It is quite tiny – on purpose' says Nicholas Holtam. 'We stand outside looking in at a scene that is at first childish and charming, but which then begins to raise serious questions. For here is God's story. Like Mother Julian's hazelnut, "it is all that is made", and when, because of its littleness, she marvels how it might last, she comes to see, "it lasts and ever shall because God loves it".'

Here is a prayer used in the communion service at St Martin's. It is for those who want to go further in their faith and for those of us who have travelled on, and wonder if we have lost our way.

'Come to this table, you who have much faith and you who would like to have more;
You who have been to this sacrament often and you who have not been for a long time;
You who have tried to follow Jesus and you who have failed.
Come, it is Christ who invites us to meet him here.'

2
GREENWICH
The Kingdom of Heaven is like… this?

*'**C**an you think of anything worse one can do to anybody than take away their worship?… without worship, you shrink, it's as brutal as that.'*

Peter Shaffer

In the tradition of a stately royal progression down the River Thames, we should have arrived at the service in the chapel of the Old Royal Naval College at a gentle and unhurried pace by water. Instead, we came by the Docklands Light Railway which, although ambling along slowly enough, unconcerned about timetables, helped to ensure that we actually arrived at a breathless trot, the closest that either of us will ever have come to running in the London Marathon. Greenwich is the backdrop for the early stages of the annual race, but on the day that we were there, the streets were full of children and dancers instead, beguiling us to linger as they celebrated an annual Festival of the Sea.

Once into the long and elegant approach to the famous Royal Naval Hospital designed by Christopher Wren, there was no time to slow down to take in 'one of the most sublime sights English architecture affords', and I had only a brief moment to thank God that the strict and lengthy security checks, in place when I escorted Sir Harry Secombe into the chapel to record a hymn for *Songs of Praise*'s friendly rival *Highway*, had now gone. A decade ago the Royal Navy had left the buildings, having occupied them since 1873 when they took over from the Royal Hospital, which had been established in 1694 for the relief and support of seamen. Today the University of Greenwich is here and, as we soon discover, some very talented musicians from Trinity College of Music.

The Chapel of Saint Peter and Saint Paul, The Old Royal Naval College, Greenwich

To the original Chapel Royal had once come a young organist and singer, Thomas Tallis, to begin in 1543 forty years of service to successive kings and queens, ensuring that he would become one of our most famous church music composers. But although the Chapel Royal was a part of Wren's plans for the whole group of buildings that have since drawn millions of tourists to the Maritime Greenwich World Heritage Site, the famous architect died before building work was finished. The plan, approved in a royal warrant signed in 1694 during the reign of William and Mary, was for a complete rebuilding of the palace where Queen Elizabeth I had been born but which in the English Civil War had been desecrated and used as a biscuit factory.

The naval pensioners first worshipped in the rebuilt chapel in 1705. The airy nave with elegant slim galleries down each side was designed in an elaborate Baroque style, but this was destroyed when fire broke out in a tailor's workshop underneath. When James Stewart and William Newton rebuilt the nave between 1779 and 1788, they kept Wren's basic shape, but decorated it in the very different Rococo style, using muted pastel colours.

The present chapel is somehow a place of beauty rather than mystery, and might feel like an elegant eighteenth-century drawing room if it were not for a huge inspirational painting over the altar by the American Benjamin West. This painting, a dramatic reminder of Paul's survival after being shipwrecked off Malta, will have set many an old sailor pondering about the dangers of life at sea and their dependence on God.

Sunday services in the chapel begin with the choir singing in the antechapel, drawn from the pool of talent at the Trinity College of Music and invisible to the congregation. With its resonant acoustics, the soaring sounds as they sang Victoria's *Jesu dulcis memoria* ('Jesus, the very thought of thee') felt like heavenly balm to us stressed latecomers.

There was to be another musical surprise later on. After communion, the choir – in their red cassocks and white surplices – sang Schubert's *Gloria* and the then chaplain, the Revd Sally Davies, sang with them from behind the altar using her own full music score. Although priests of the Anglican Church are expected to be able to sing, I have never before seen a priest play a full part in the complicated setting of a Schubert Mass. It was a strangely moving experience and broke down my prejudices about choirs and preachers living on different planets to one another.

We had come to Greenwich because Tricia Camisotti, a listener to GLR – the BBC's radio station for London and one of the local radio stations where I had asked for suggestions for the nation's favourite churches – had nominated the chapel. After the service, with the help of the chaplain and the congregation, we were able to experience the kindness and hospitality of the chapel community and find Tricia. It wasn't difficult because she was serving the tea and coffee after the service. Tricia first came as a tourist to look at the building, but now says that it is her spiritual home. And yet, as we discovered, you don't have to make the coffee for a large congregation to belong to this very friendly and diverse community.

The writer Cesare Pavese says that we do not remember days – we remember moments. And that is how we remember our visit to the chapel in Greenwich. Because we were latecomers, we sat in a pew right by the door and it was only because we were there that we could glimpse one of our best 'moments'.

The chapel's acoustics are ideal not only for both medieval and baroque music, but also in ensuring that a tearful baby's cries can be heard everywhere, as in this instance. Whilst the chaplain battled on in the pulpit through squeals of both joy and protest, we became more attentive to her sermon once the little child had been taken out. I always feel relieved at such moments but also slightly guilty, for surely in such

children lies the kingdom of heaven? We were about to see. After the sermon, her father tried to return swiftly, discreetly and invisibly back to his pew with a now content child, but he did not have a chance. Carried high on his shoulders as they re-entered the chapel, he probably never even knew that from her lofty height, his daughter gave the whole congregation a huge happy wave, as the choir were singing 'Blessed is he that cometh in the name of the Lord'.

We would also not forget the 'Home Group' psalm, which was said during the service. You will not recognize it as a rewritten version of the 150 Psalms of David nor find it in the Prayer Book under Psalm 151. This is a psalm written by different members of the chapel congregation who meet to study and pray in their homes. Each person had contributed their own verse and although the unique personalities come through, you will probably also recognize yourself, as I did myself.

Just as the storms of war at sea must have been familiar to the old sea dog pensioners who once worshipped here under the huge painting of the shipwreck of Paul, all our storms of life are now shared in

The Home Group Psalm

1　O Lord my God,
　　In thee do I put my trust.

2　I come to you in sorrow, gracious Lord;
　　lift my burdens and let me see your greatness.

3　On you, Lord, I fix my hope;
　　you, Lord my God, will answer.

4　O Lord, in times of need, of distress and despair,
　　let me turn to you in prayer and ask for help,
　　your comfort and compassion.

5　Have mercy upon me, O Lord,
　　for I am weak in faith and need to be stronger.

6　Thou hast set my feet in a large belly;
　　have mercy upon me, O Lord, for I am in trouble.

7　May those who live in fear, dominated by fanaticism,
　　be freed by your love.

8　O Lord, have mercy upon me,
　　for I have a strong tendency to make judgements
　　upon others,

9　but you have delivered me from suffocation
　　and restored me to breathe anew!

10　Far from me, yet within me, companion, still
　　awaited, deeply known unknowable, God, my God!

The painting by Benjamin West of the shipwreck of Paul dominates the chapel interior

this psalm. It is written by people who have not just brought a new lease of life to this famous and beautiful building, but who are also helping to build the kingdom of heaven.

As we left the chapel and its friendly community, we found ourselves once more in the streets of Greenwich, which had now been turned into a beach, with vast sandpits stretching along the pavements. In one of these sandpits, a man was building a beautiful sand sculpture of a prancing horse, whilst all around him children were making their own sandcastles and carrying around sandy buckets of water. Of such is the kingdom of heaven.

17

3
THAXTED
Mingling Heaven and Earth

*'**T**haxted is becoming a place of pilgrimage for those who are tired of the sluggish routine and conventionalism of much modern Nonconformity and of the "C of E". Yet we are proud to claim membership in the Church of England for she is the Church of Anselm and of Becket and of John Ball who fought for the freedom of the people.'*

Conrad Noel, vicar of Thaxted, 1918

Sunday afternoon in rural north Essex. The church clock stands at ten to six. An almost cloudless summer sky is silent and empty. The view looking down the main street could be the opening scene in a light opera set in merrie England. Cottages frame the set and at its centre, there is the Guildhall, a beautiful half-timbered building begun in 1390. Although the tentacles of London's ever-increasing suburban sprawl are not that far away, there is nothing to suggest that the tranquillity will ever be disturbed… except for a rash of nearby roadside signs ominously protesting *'No to Stansted Airport's Second Runway!'*

Thaxted, however, is ready for visitors. Not only are the tea shops open, but waiters in white aprons are standing at the door ready to greet the thirsty traveller. It is hard to believe that this idyllic scene is not a dream, for most tea shops in English country towns usually start to pile chairs on tables as soon as the hour of four strikes. *Songs of Praise* producers, pausing from rehearsals at teatime, have long learned to do without such indulgences as finding a café open – except when visiting Thaxted.

But even the finest tea room cannot distract me from heading for the parish church, whose tower and spire dominate the town, and where once the vicar preached revolution.

The Church of St John the Baptist with Our Lady and St Laurence, Thaxted

Thaxted Parish Church dates from the fourteenth century and its construction took almost 200 years. The tower is as high as the church is long and a surprisingly narrow nave is surrounded by wide aisles.

Inside, angels and saints look down on worshippers whilst outside, snarling gargoyles help deposit rain falling on the roof onto the heads of visitors in the churchyard. There are only a few chairs in the church, and so it is possible to imagine the medieval setting, when only the 'weak went to the wall' and sat on ledges along the sides. There is a fine seventeenth-century pulpit and an extraordinary font case and cover from the fifteenth century. For the Songs of Praise producer, this is a dream of a church. A substantial organ, architecture of great beauty wherever the cameras point, and huge spaces to conceal even the largest TV technology from the viewers' eyes.

The medieval building is a wonder in its own right, but many people come here to find out more about one of the most revolutionary clergymen of recent times, Conrad Noel, vicar of Thaxted for more than thirty years. Just one sentence that he wrote in 1918 is sufficient to introduce this forthright characte. 'My objective must be to encourage the rising of the people in the might of the Risen Christ and the Saints, mingling Heaven and Earth, that we shatter this greedy world to bits.'

This Sunday, Thaxted is slumbering. The spacious church is cool but full of sunlight. Many of the windows are of plain glass, and my first impression is of being inside a medieval summer house, but it seems to be giving off a holy aura to the other visitors scattered around the building. They speak to each other in whispers and tiptoe across the medieval flagstones, as if ancient monks are kneeling in prayer in some distant corner of this vast building.

Alas, there is no sign of impending evensong, and so we all continue to wander. If there are church watchers here, I cannot see them. Then, turning past a pillar in the south aisle, I am confronted with a face. It is Conrad Noel – or at least his bust cast in bronze, his eyes fixed on the visitor. The spirit of the man, once such a strong presence here, seems to be waiting to remind me, the languid tourist, of my duties to both God and to the poor.

Turning away, I feel another pair of eyes, gazing unblinking across the church at the former vicar's frozen features. It is a fierce hawk, on the most startling lectern that I have ever come across. The painted and carved wooden eagle, on whose wings the open Bible was read to Noel's congregation and preached by him as a manifesto for revolution, is unnervingly eyeballing me from its perch on what looks like a small maypole.

Whatever was Conrad Noel doing in 1918 in a quiet, old-fashioned village where caps were still doffed to the aristocracy?

One of the greatest supporters of Noel's gospel of Christian Socialism was herself an aristocrat. Daisy, Countess of Warwick, one of Edwardian society's most dazzling beauties, had had a passionate affair with the Prince of Wales before he became King Edward VII. But Daisy also had a passion for revolutionary ideas, and was the patron of Thaxted Church. This gave her the right to choose the vicar and in 1910, at the height of the golden age of Edwardian society, she wrote to a friend, 'Conrad Noel has accepted a living of mine in Thaxted; such a beautiful cathedral-church, and we must make it a centre and a Mecca for Socialists!' She may have intended that Noel would pursue his revolutionary writing from the vicarage, however, and let parish life continue on its sleepy course, but that was not to be.

In Noel's day, church services at Thaxted were as revolutionary as the vicar's thinking. There were processions with the clergy in 'coats of many colours',

children waving flowers and branches, and men with flaming torches and banners. Noel would set hymns to Gilbert and Sullivan opera music (a forerunner to the 'crossover' music featured now on *Songs of Praise*), and he would preach using the symbolism of fairy stories. His wife Miriam led the revival of English country dancing, and morris dancers were encouraged to perform in the church.

Another person who first came to the area in 1913 also left his mark on the wider world. As war with Germany was declared, Mr Gustav von Holst's presence in Thaxted was regarded with suspicion by the local policeman. But Mr 'Von', as Noel and his parishioners called him, was composing one of the world's all-time favourites, 'The Planets' suite. The tune for the planet Venus has become even better known as the hymn tune 'Thaxted'.

Gustav Holst organized a Whitsun festival, in which all the music was performed within the services in the parish church. His daughter, Imogen, the conductor and composer, said that the singing used to go on for hour after hour. Her father played the organ for the Christmas services, but it is for Whitsun that he wrote the chorus, 'Our church bells in Thaxted at Whitsuntide say, "Come all you good people and put care away".' Inscribed on one of Thaxted's own church bells are the words 'I ring for the General Dance', a reminder of another of Holst's well-known compositions, dedicated to his friend Conrad Noel – a setting of the carol 'Tomorrow shall be my dancing day'.

Conrad Noel wanted to preach Christ present at communion, the common meal, with the 'useful bread' and the 'genial wine' being shared as a prelude to 'the New World Order in which all would be justly produced and distributed'. Perhaps not surprisingly, at a time when even a weekly parish communion was regarded as revolutionary, many regarded the vicar with suspicion. Never more so than in the row about the three flags.

Flying together the flag of St George of England with the Tricolour of the Irish Republic and the Red Flag of the Russian Revolution would raise eyebrows even today. But to understand why such a national fuss was made in 1918, we need to remember that for the first time ever, the whole world was at war and men had gone from Thaxted to fight in the trenches. Today, on the wall of the tower, a long list still records the names of those who did not return. At the height of this terrible war, on Easter

Day 1916, an uprising had begun in Ireland and finally in 1917, revolution came to Russia. What then, in the middle of such apocalyptic ferment, was a Church of England clergyman trying to tell his flock?

The vicar claimed that he had been given the Sinn Fein tricolour by an Irish lady living in the parish. He already had the St George's flag, which still flies on many English churches to this day. What better then, said Noel, than 'to add to these national flags the International, in which the Variety in Unity and the Unity in Variety, the very nature of the God who created the universe, should be worshipped'?

So up went the Red Flag.

Whether Noel was naïve or whether he anticipated a good fight, we shall never know. But in the following months and years, Thaxted and its vicar gained notoriety around the world, and the goings-on were even published in Moscow newspapers.

The flags were torn down and burnt and replaced by the Union Jack, which Noel then pulled down and destroyed. Raiding parties descended on the church, armed first with ladders and then cudgels. Flags went up and down, and the Red Flag was even sent to the bishop, who rebuked his priest and passed the flag to Scotland Yard. The vicar was reported to the War Office as a traitor, and the matter was raised in the House of Commons. However, nobody ever discovered a law that he had broken.

One day in 1926, thousands of demonstrators came to hold a protest rally in the Guildhall, during which time the vicar's supporters (he had by then won over many of his congregation) let the invaders' car tyres down. Finally, a posse of burly ex-policemen, who supported Noel, but had since lost their jobs for going

Conrad Noel 1869–1942, vicar of Thaxted

on strike, fought off the mob as they threatened to destroy the church.

This colourful episode at Thaxted was but a tiny skirmish in a battle of ideas. When Conrad Noel died in July 1942, the world was once again at war. The social change that he had so fervently prayed for had come about not in peace but in the

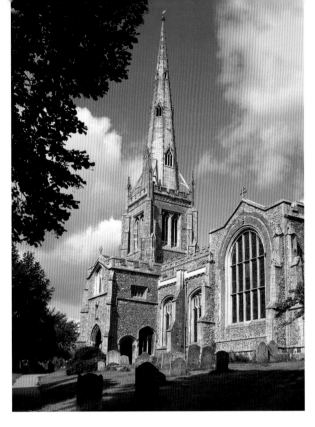

most tragic circumstances through another world war. Once again, both rich and poor faced hardship and death together in a desperate struggle to free the world of terrible tyranny.

On a summer's day, the vicar's body was borne into Thaxted Church. Even the vicarage dog was there. The church singers, who had been trained years before by Gustav Holst, sang. Miriam Noel, her daughter and granddaughter, together with the churchwardens and the whole church family, shared communion, Noel's beloved 'common meal'.

Afterwards at the grave, words were spoken that might have been written about him:

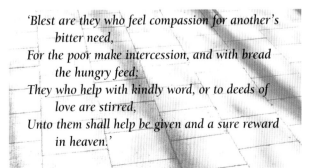

*'Blest are they who feel compassion for another's bitter need,
For the poor make intercession, and with bread the hungry feed;
They who help with kindly word, or to deeds of love are stirred,
Unto them shall help be given and a sure reward in heaven.'*

4

WOOD WALTON

By the Way

'In the afternoon between Stamford and Stilton there was a young unruly horse in the chaise which ran away with the driver, and jumping to one side of the road, we were overturned. We got a pretty severe rap. However, we got up and pursued our way. During our last two stages, which we travelled in the dark, I was a good deal afraid of robbers. A great many horrid ideas filled my mind. However I affected resolution, and as each of us carried a loaded pistol in his hand, we were pretty secure.'

from Boswell's London Journey, *15 November 1762*

There is a little church which hundreds of travellers pass every day. It stands beside a busy railway line, an ancient landmark in the passing scenery that many may notice as the express rushes them past, but few will ever visit.

When the diarist James Boswell travelled from Edinburgh to London in 1762 to meet Dr Johnson, his future travelling companion, the journey took four days. These days, my own journey between the two capitals takes four hours. But this is no ordinary commute. Starting under the lantern tower of St Giles' Cathedral, the High Kirk of Edinburgh, the story of more than 1,000 years of

James Boswell 1740–1795.
Lawyer, diarist and travelling
companion to Dr Johnson

Christian Britain unfolds through the carriage window. After Holy Island, and the land of the Northumbrian saints, Aidan, Bede and Cuthbert, the sleek express rushes on past some of England's most outstandingly beautiful churches and cathedrals. I am amazed that so few people look.

The halfway point on the journey to London is marked by the huge tower of St George's Church in Doncaster, a church where in 1790 an organist first introduced an experience familiar to *Songs of Praise* participants, a hymn singing rehearsal. 'The eminent Dr Miller announces that he will be present at the organ every Wednesday to give instruction in singing.'

It seems that today, there is no time for business travellers even to glance up from their laptops at St George's nor, as we travel further south, at St Wulfram's in Grantham, whose Gothic spire caused the Victorian artist, John Ruskin, to swoon when he first saw it from the train.

South of Huntingdon we cross the meadows by the River Nene and pass Godmanchester Parish Church, where in 1976 the very first *Songs of Praise* was made in which a community chose their favourite hymns. In fact, *Songs of Praise* has come from many of the churches and cathedrals that have flashed by on this journey. But there is one little church where the programme has never been, and we pass it during one of the high-speed parts of the journey.

Travelling at more than two miles a minute, there are only a few seconds to see a break in the wide open fields and catch a glimpse of a small graveyard surrounding a church with a sturdy tower. This little church has always intrigued me as it seems to stand entirely alone in the fields. Does anyone worship there? At first light on a winter's morning, I have even wondered if it was some sort of mirage, a ghost from a simpler rural age, visible only to exhausted travellers trying to wake up for a hard day's work in London. Now I have an excuse to explore, for I think it may be eligible to become one of the nation's favourite churches, if only because it offers a few seconds of beauty and peace to the thousands of rail passengers who pass by daily.

The church is St Andrew's, Wood Walton, and I discover that it is only a couple of miles off the A1, the Great North Road, near Stilton in Cambridgeshire, where one afternoon in the eighteenth century Boswell's chaise overturned. There aren't any signs to a church in the village of Wood Walton, but a signpost with its arm broken off offers a clue. Passing through a narrow lane winds through fields of corn and suddenly, there it is.

There is no road to the church, just an old green lane protected by a gate, through which even a thin walker has to squeeze. The grassy track skirts a copse from which a peacock calls. A train rushes by and disrupts the

perfect stillness for just a few seconds. But quickly I find myself alone again in the silence with the little building that keeps watch over miles of fenland. I have stepped out of the rush hour into the past.

In the sun-filled south porch, there are two notices on the locked door: one announces that the church is cared for by the Friends of Friendless Churches, and the other, more mysteriously, states that 'No mowers or gardening implements are kept in this church'.

The Parish Church of St Andrew's, Wood Walton

There is a church in Wood Walton recorded in the Domesday Book of 1086, but possibly not on this site. The present building began with a simple nave and a chancel to which the south aisle was added around 1250. Since then, a lot of building, rebuilding and modifications have taken place. The north aisle and the tower were added in the fourteenth

century, then rebuilt, and a clerestory was added early in the sixteenth century.

Between 1856 and 1859, the Victorians ordered a makeover, hiding so much of what had survived the turbulent centuries of English church history. Enthused with the zeal for Gothic Revival, they used 'state-of-the-art technology', replacing the craft of the medieval mason with machined stone and replica windows as well as rebuilding the tower. In 1897, 1906 and 1911, further 'improvements' were made. As a result, St Andrew's does not even rate a mention in Betjeman's Guide, although if John Mason Neale or Daniel Defoe had found their way here, they would probably have been in favour of the refurbishments. Tourists may now travel the world and find solace in beautiful ruins, but both these guides would have described such sights as 'melancholy'. For Defoe, a new church steeple was a sign of prosperity and of 'decency and convenience'. Neale, by contrast, wanted to see 'reverence and holiness' expressed in the reconstruction of a lost age - the world of medieval art and faith through the architecture of the Gothic age. But in neither man's view could things be left as they were.

The little building may have always stood apart from the village, because thieves were up to no good here long before the age of the mower, and as early as 1549 an account records, 'Woddwaltton stoln out of the Church... ii handbells.'

Usually there is some reason for a church to be so isolated. Sometimes a plague, especially the Black Death in the fourteenth century, has led to a church being abandoned as the community vanished. Sometimes wealthy farming landowners preferred to tidy the inhabitants out of the way into a new village elsewhere. The churches remain.

So what has this redundant church to say to us travellers now as we dash past, in fear of our own redundancy? Is this the last remnant of a wiser, slower paced world that we now find ourselves permanently cut off from? Is it the past we are looking for when we visit old churches? Should we wish that world back?

In February 1951, with preparations underway for The Festival of Britain in London, Life magazine – in a paean of praise for the new age of science and discovery – chose to devote an entire page for its American readers on a feature about an old lady in her cottage in rural England. Mrs Fanny Thorne, eighty-eight-years-old, was photographed making tea in her kitchen. The writer saw it as symbolic of the British way of life – the table covered with utilitarian oilcloth and chairs offering a 'certain slovenly comfort'. There was the cat and the radio and the table from where children and grandchildren were fed. It was a timeless image, like an ancient church viewed from a high-speed train.

'Her life has been marked with deliberate sameness. At eleven, she went to work in her father's field. It was in the local church where she sang in the village choir, that she became the bride of a village soldier boy. When her husband went to the Boer War, she took to working the land again to feed her children.'

Her husband had died in the Great War, but almost forty years later, *Life* wrote, 'From that day to this, save only Sunday, Fanny Thorne has gone every morning to the fields as a hired hand,' and worked 'threshing wheat, sorting potatoes or cutting kale for the cattle. At the age of eighty-six, the great grandmother of nineteen has "stooked" an eight-acre field of barley by herself in eleven and a half hours.'

The larks are singing invisibly in the cloudless sky above St Andrew's as I look at the headstones on the graves in the churchyard. Some are indecipherable, and covered with lichen, but others can be read and clearly mark the resting places of all the Fanny Thornes of Wood Walton, offering rest for people after a lifetime which was not full of 'olde worlde' charm but instead hard and insecure, and where they really did go hungry. I certainly wouldn't wish this world back.

It does not matter that there is no one to ask about St Andrew's, nor even that I cannot go in. The experience of just being here on this summer afternoon will do. These stones that survive only through the good offices of the Friends of Friendless Churches are a meditation in themselves.

Every year, St Andrew's Church opens for a harvest festival service, with a full house and traditional hymns. But the prayers are not from the past but for today, for farming as it is now and for the world as it might become.

The church by the railway at Wood Walton, itself a prayer set in stone, seems to wish us well on our journeys into the future. On the other side of the earth, in New Zealand, the Revd Bill Marsh, a retired farmer, does the same. He offers this prayer for us as we all travel on our way.

'May you see God's light on the path ahead
When the road you walk is dark.
May you always hear,
Even in your hour of sorrow,
The gentle singing of the lark.
When times are hard may hardness
Never turn your heart to stone.
May you always remember
When the shadows fall
You do not walk alone.'

5

WALPOLE

An Odour of Comfort, Sweetness and Grace

'*May thy blessing, O Lord, descend upon this incense or frankincense, as on that of which thy prophet David sang, saying, let my prayer be set forth in thy sight as the incense; let it be unto us as an odour of comfort, sweetness and grace; that by its fumes every illusion of the enemy, of mind and body, may be put to flight; that we may be, in the words of the apostle Paul, a sweet savour unto God. Before the face of this incense or frankincense let every assault of devils flee away, as dust before the face of the wind, and as smoke before the face of the fire.'*

from 'Sabbatum Sanctum', the Service for Easter Even in the Sarum Missal, *1526*

Hidden among the trees on the edge of the marshland of west Norfolk, out of earshot but not far from one of East Anglia's busiest roads, is one of the twelve most famous parish churches in England. As far as I can discover, this ancient and holy parish church of Walpole St Peter, a known favourite of the heir to the throne, has never been the setting for a BBC broadcast. However, John Betjeman called it the finest of all and it has also been described as an act of worship in itself.

As I pushed open the ancient door of an apparently empty Walpole Church, I was surprised to be greeted by the sweet smell of incense. In medieval England, it would have been a familiar smell, its smoke a symbol of ascending prayer, used originally in the Jewish Temple and from the ninth century in the Christian church. Only once was I made responsible for the incense at a service. It is an acquired art, one which I did not acquire, first nearly asphyxiating myself as the 'holy smoke' billowed uncontrollably in the vestry, but then when the fire was out, presenting the thurible to the rector.

Although becoming a rarer event, incense is still used in some church services but there was something different here: there wasn't a soul in sight. Speeding towards the altar, I expected to find a forgotten thurible, the handheld brass container in which it burns, still smoking on its stand. Churches have caught fire because of neglected lit candles or incense. Perhaps I was intruding on the private prayer of some holy priest, trained in the art when some parishes still had enough curates to field a cricket team, but now forgetful and alone on his knees. But not only was there no one else in the church, there was also no obvious source for the smell. And yet it hung heavily in the air, like the building's own welcome and an invitation to travel back 600 years to medieval England.

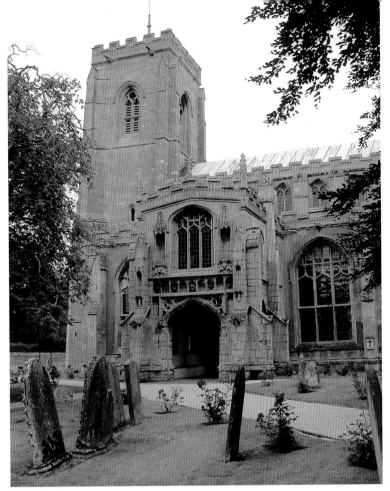

The Parish Church of St Peter's, Walpole St Peter

Although the village is linked to King's Lynn and the busy industries of modern north-west Norfolk, its church is a northern outpost of the Diocese of Ely. Far to the south stands the mother church, the cathedral of Ely, a once great centre of Christianity in medieval times. So Walpole St Peter belongs to the Fen Country, the flat, mist-filled country of 'drowns' – the sudden devastating floods coming in off the North Sea, trying to recapture the land man has taken, engulfing the scattered homes and farms in the process.

Nearly 700 years ago, one such flood was followed by plague as the Black Death quickly killed off half the local population. All that remained in Walpole was its late thirteenth-century church tower. But the people of East Anglia fought back, and by the fifteenth century an immense new church – 160 feet in length – had been built using red sandstone. Here, for a century, the souls of its dead benefactors would be prayed for.

Even by East Anglian standards, with its many great churches, Walpole St Peter is impressive. For another 100 years, the building grew even further, extending right up to the eastern boundary of the graveyard. It was the time of the 'Sarum Rite', the prayer book of Pre-Reformation England with its ornate ceremonies. There is still an arched passageway under the chancel, called the 'Good Friday Way', where once solemn processions circled the church before the lighting of the huge Easter candle and the blessing of incense – 'the odour of comfort, sweetness and grace'.

In the aisles are enormous, richly-decorated fifteenth-century benches, but if the many large windows in a perpendicular style and the battlements and impressive porches are reminders of its medieval Gothic origins, most of the interior of Walpole Church has a seventeenth-century Jacobean feel. Across the west end of the nave is a delicate screen through which visitors pass into a space filled with silvery-coloured oak pews lit by a chandelier made in 1701. Apart from the saints carved on the portion of the medieval rood screen that survives, other icons and statues have been replaced by monuments to the great and the good from the intervening ages. At the east end, twenty-one steps lead up to the altar in the chancel, the only part of the church 'restored' by the Victorians. For once, they were unusually sensitive.

Yet Walpole Church is no mausoleum, but instead a space where the work of unknown carpenters and masons still inspires a village, and visitors come from across the world.

'I am happy to talk to you, but you won't get me before Thursday, because I am out building.' The Revd Mike Chesher, the clerk in holy orders responsible for the care of the souls of the parish, is anxious that he should not be pigeonholed. This priest is not only a qualified bricklayer, but has previously worked in engineering and in the newspaper industry. The country parish may appear traditional, but it often seems to be adapting itself to change more effectively than many a suburban church.

For Mike, who first felt the call to be a priest when he was eleven years old, it was to be another thirty years before he started conversations with the church, and a further twelve months before he began three years of part-time training for ordination at Westcott House in Cambridge. 'It was quite scary, especially as I thought that I had failed in my very first interview.'

'He is a gift from God,' says Anne Clery-Fox, one of his parishioners. 'I think it's like going home being at his services. And there is a lot of laughter so you don't slumber in the pews. "How well do you know your Bible?" he will suddenly ask us, breaking off in the sermon. Or "who was the male financial genius who kept all his assets on board whilst the rest went into liquidation?"' I am stumped.

Having heard about the lively services, I am almost certain that my incense experience must have been imagined. But Anne denies this, saying that 'we are reverent in Walpole and we have William, who has been here for yonks, to do the incense every Sunday, and besides – the bats like it!'

I later come across an extraordinary story about incense that appeared in *The Listener* magazine in 1940. 'A listener with great enthusiasm for BBC broadcasts describes how, when the local station was out of action, a small boy begged his mother to burn incense in front of the radio as he had seen her doing in front of Icons of the Saints. After her pious act, she turned the knob of the radio and a voice was heard to say: "Goodnight from London". Now, the boy stands at attention every night and salutes the transmission.'

It is a reminder of how to listeners in wartime, the Corporation was the voice of freedom and hope, the 'odour of comfort, sweetness and grace' of the airwaves.

An early seventeenth–century poorbox. Today, a number of them survive. Money paid to a church by the wealthy to have prayers said to commemorate dead family members would be given to the poor

The Revd Mike Chesher, vicar of St Peter's, Walpole St Peter

6

DALTON HOLME
A Work of Noble Seriousness

'I hope that the minister, to whom the custody of the church key belongs, will take care that one is kept near the church. It is a very tiresome thing, when one has come a long way to see a church, to find that the clerk lives a mile off, and when you get to his cottage hot and tired, to hear that he has gone out, and taken the key with him.'

from A Few Words to Churchwardens *by John Mason Neale, 1843*

From the northern tip of Lincolnshire, the modern traveller arrives easily in the East Riding of Yorkshire via the Humber [suspension] Bridge, taking only a minute or two to cross. In Daniel Defoe's day, however, a ferryman had to be hired for what could be a long and dangerous crossing. Defoe noticed the contrast between the two sides of the River Humber in his diary, writing that Hull 'tis extraordinarily populous, even to an inconvenience… and there are but two churches'; Lincoln, on the other hand, 'is an ancient, ragged, decay'd city; it is so full of ruins of monasteries and religious houses, that in short, the very barns, stables and as they showed me, some of the pig-styes, were built church-fashion.'

Songs of Praise discovered through the recording of two programmes at The Minster that these days the churches of Lincolnshire flourish.

Meanwhile, the Humber Bridge now leads the motorist not only to Hull but also to

Beverley, with its outstandingly beautiful medieval Minster. Only a few miles further on into Yorkshire, there is a sight that would have gladdened Defoe's eyes. To him a fine spire defined a fine church and here, at Dalton Holme, is one of the finest spires in the whole of Britain.

'Jerusalem the golden
With milk and honey blest
Beneath thy contemplation
Sink heart and mind at rest.
I know not, oh I know not
What joys await me there,
What radiancy of glory
What light beyond compare.'

from Jerusalem the Golden, *Bernard of Cluny, c. twelfth century,*
translated by John Mason Neale and others

The Parish Church of St Mary's, Dalton Holme

The church was commissioned by Lord Hotham, a wealthy landowner on whose land it was built in 1858. The family still live nearby and the present Lord Hotham is churchwarden. The original cost was £25,000 and it would be fascinating to know how much of this was spent on the slender steeple that is 208 feet high and so well designed that there are no buttresses. The base of the spire is octagonal and sits so perfectly on the equally slim tower that our eyes are drawn naturally up to the sky. By contrast, the nave is quite short, but the small cruciform interior still has a feeling of spaciousness. The church dominates the short village street and its nearby almshouses.

The buildings designed by John Loughborough Pearson have been described as works of 'noble seriousness' and it seems that the experience of growing up in the city of Durham, in the shadow of England's most formidable Norman cathedral, had made its mark.

Pearson was actually born in Brussels in 1817, the son of a watercolour painter. He began his training as an architect at the age of fourteen. Although he excelled with designs, such as the spire for South Dalton, he was not viewed a success with church fittings like the altar, and in his first church design even forgot to leave room for the organ. He was described as 'a middle-of-the-road Anglican, a Christian who didn't make a fuss about it and neither effusive nor provocative in personality'. But he excelled at creating spacious interiors using the Gothic style, whose revival so preoccupied many wilder Victorian architects. Pearson designed St Augustine's Kilburn (1871), St George's Cullercoats (1882) and Holy Trinity in Ayr (1886), all of which have been featured on Songs of Praise. His biggest project was the design of Truro Cathedral, begun in 1880.

Although John Betjeman thought it 'rather prickly' in its detail, he underlined St Mary's as a 'must-visit' church, and a listener to Radio Humberside nominated it as a nation's favourite. But it was by pure chance that we stumbled upon it. Driving along a road through empty countryside, I glimpsed just for a second a tall spire rising above woods. I didn't even slow down. Earlier in the year, on another journey for a *Songs of Praise* book, I suddenly had the distinct impression of a medieval cathedral with gleaming spires towering across the winter countryside. It was a hallucination, as it didn't exist and I thought that this was yet another mirage. But my wife Liz spotted a small handwritten notice by the roadside: 'our beautiful church is open today. Welcome.' I slowed down and the spire reappeared, but always tantalizingly out of reach across fields, and etched against a bright evening sky. Would it still be open when we finally completed a series of tortuous circuits across winding byroads?

Fortunately, there are still people – in this case the twenty-seven members on the electoral roll of St Mary's – who trust others and leave their beautiful church, with its doors wide open, unlocked most hours in order to welcome the stranger. On the sunny evening that we were there, there was not another soul to be seen anywhere in the church or even in the village. All there was were two 'middle-of-the-road Anglicans', privileged and inspired by this surprising gem, courtesy of the Creator and his nineteenth-century agent, Pearson. An earlier visitor had written in the visitor's book, 'This is I think what Aunt Mary calls heaven.'

*'They stand, those halls of Sion,
all jubilant with song
and bright with many an angel
and all the martyr throng;
the Prince is ever with them,
the daylight is serene
the pastures of the blessed
are decked in glorious sheen.'*

from Jerusalem the Golden, *Bernard of Cluny, c. twelfth century, translated by John Mason Neale and others*

7
YORK
A Kind of Inspiration

'*The varied tones, sometimes low, sometimes swelling into a great volume of harmonised sound, seemed to anticipate the songs of the blessed and the chorus of praise round the throne of God.*'

William Richardson, vicar of St Michael-le-Belfrey, describing the sound of evensong in York Minster

The story of St Michael-le-Belfrey is inextricably linked with that of its big sister and next door neighbour, York Minster, the mother church of the Anglican Province of York and today the seat of Britain's first black archbishop, John Sentamu.

But perhaps it was the above description of evensong at the Minster by a well-respected man, known as the 'Father of the York clergy', that tempted the famous Victorian hymn writer, John Mason Neale, to visit York. For fifty years, Revd William Richardson had been vicar of the little church which stands next door and had often led services at the Minster. But Richardson died in 1821 and by 1843, when John Mason Neale descended on the city in time to hear the cathedral bell ringing for vespers, standards had clearly slipped:

'*What a miserable thing is an afternoon service in York Minster! I wonder that such continual coming in and going out of the choir in the middle of service, such irreverence, such lolling, or rather lying down on the forms, are not felt to be a disgrace. To make the thing perfect, half a dozen sofas should be put in the middle of the choir, and placarded: "For the accommodation of visitors" and then the profanity would hardly exceed the present.*'

A Church Tour through England and Wales *by John Mason Neale*

In Neale's day, vergers made a meagre living mainly from tourists, and in York Minster there was an odd custom that visitors, whilst forbidden to enter the empty nave during services, were often escorted into the quire and shown round. A local newspaper fulminated, 'For too long has vergerdom sat like a dark dragon at the porch of God's house in the obscure watch for sixpences.'

Neale sustained his gloomy mood by finishing his first day with a visit to the nearby Battle of Marston Moor site. A century and a half earlier, after travelling to York and finding the Minster 'in want of a fine spire', Daniel Defoe had enjoyed visiting Marston Moor, where he had met a survivor of the English Civil War. But Neale found 'nothing to see' until glimpsing a beautiful sunset whilst on a train, setting off thought about 'hope through immortality'. Which was the most striking representation of that hope – this sunset or the cathedral that he had just visited and found in such a profane state?

Back in York, Neale visited St Michael-le-Belfrey, which he described as 'the swansong of English Gothic architecture'. In fact it was the last ever church built in the Gothic style in England. His mood improved

John Mason Neale, 1818–1866. Anglican priest and hymn-writer

considerably, and even if York Minster still did not gain from Neale the accolade that Defoe had given it as 'the beautifullest Church', he did conclude that 'hope through immortality' lay behind such a creation. Genius, he wrote, was not an adequate description, and nothing short of 'a kind of inspiration' could have produced York

Minster. Just as Italian painters would not attempt painting a Madonna without first receiving Holy Communion, only an architect in such a divinely inspired frame of mind 'could conceive and perfect such ideas'.

It was just such a man who designed the little church that, as one recent guide wrote, 'crouches humbly beside the Minster'. The man given a 'kind of inspiration' to design and build St Michael-le-Belfrey was John Foreman. He was the very last of a line of medieval architects and master masons of York Minster.

The Parish Church of St Michael-le-Belfrey, York

Like the Minster, the church – a simple box-like structure with slender pillars separating the nave from the aisles - was built on the cruciform foundations of the headquarters of Roman York, where in AD 306 Constantine the Great was proclaimed Emperor. By the seventh century, a stone church had been built on the site of the present Minster, and by the thirteenth century, a small chapel stood where St Michael's now stands and provided a quiet space for worship away from the splendour of the medieval cathedral.

The thirteenth-century chapel was ruined and neglected when John Foreman began work in 1525. St Michael's came into being at a time when churches were more likely to be destroyed as Henry VIII stripped power and wealth from the clergy and then the Reformers tore down much of what had survived that purge. In the nave floor of Foreman's church is a fifteen-foot long stone edged pre-Reformation carving. Could this be the high altar of the medieval Minster, which in 1568 was 'struck down' by order of Archbishop Grindal and replaced by a wooden table?

Perhaps the most famous person to come to St Michael's was brought here from his home in a nearby street

Sixteenth-century glass showing St George and the dragon

to be baptized on 16 April 1570. Guye, son of Mr Edward Fawkes, grew up to be the ringleader of the Gunpowder Plot, an event that was thwarted on 5 November 1605. Many people whose lives revolved around the Minster are buried here, including Jane Hodgson, wife of Phineas, chancellor of the Minster from 1625–41. Fourteen of the twenty-four children that she gave birth to were also baptized here.

The stained glass in the east window shows the resurrection and is all that survives from the original thirteenth-century chapel. The glass in the north aisle windows was rescued from a nearby church demolished in 1585, and one of the windows depicts St Michael, patron saint of the church, fighting with a dragon; the south aisle glass was all made in the 1530s by a Flemish glazier, John Almayne, using coloured enamels. Look out especially for St George in combat with another dragon, and St Christopher, patron saint of travellers and visitors.

Behind the altar is an eighteenth-century reredos into which in 1926 was placed a painting of the adoration of the shepherds at the manger in Bethlehem.

Sitting on the pavement halfway between the Minster and St Michael-le-Belfrey, a young man is busking with a penny whistle. As always, the great west door of the Minster beckons me, but as soon as I turn in that direction, the musician breaks into a show-stopping performance of 'Amazing Grace'. I duly change course and make for St Michael-le-Belfrey.

The service on a Sunday often begins with singing outside on the pavement. Sometimes a paddling pool is placed outside the door so that passers-by can join the congregation at a baptism service. St Michael-le-Belfrey always seems to be open for business, even when the great wooden west doors of the towering Minster next door are closed. Even late in the evening, I have been offered a brief guide to the Christian faith by someone who appeared to be only recently out of primary school.

Today, as I sit at the back of the nave, a couple from North America pause by my pew to read the notice asking that people fill up the seats from the far end first so that latecomers can find a place. The woman seems entranced by this. 'This must be a Methodist Church!' she exclaims. No. But this is the Church of England with a difference, where the congregation does not sit as far from each other as possible, or welcome the stranger with the warning that they are 'sitting in someone's seat'.

Between services, St Michael's retains a calm and relaxing atmosphere, so much so that I don't even notice at first a little gathering in the large space in front of the altar. It begins with unostentatious prayers, in which I feel able to share, but which also acts as my excuse for listening in to the conversation that follows. They are talking about the language used in the services for the Chinese community within the area, and how St Michael's could try to provide for both Cantonese and Mandarin worshippers. The answer is, it seems, 'can do'. I am immediately given a whole new insight into praying for the needs of the world. How many churches could even say 'welcome' in any other language? No wonder that the motto of St Michael's is 'Bring in – build up – send out'.

When *Songs of Praise* came from St Michael's on Easter Day 1974, they had more than one reason to celebrate. Until 1973 the church had been facing closure. But eight years earlier, a remarkable new Anglican priest had arrived in York, to be vicar at St Cuthbert's, a tiny church nearby. David Watson's preaching, like William Richardson's in the eighteenth century, filled churches to the brim, including York Minster. When he then became vicar of St Michael's in the early seventies, it received new life.

David Watson died in 1984, having faced his own death with an inspirational courage and faith, and his work in York will always be remembered for the sowing of seeds in a truly profound way.

Today St Michael's has over 700 members and three services every Sunday as well as offering daily weekday worship. St Cuthbert's is also included, having a new role as a centre for multimedia worship for a generation that 'does not do church'.

The harmonious relationships that exists today within this little parish church, with its formidable big sister, has been the continuation of a story that began almost 500 years earlier through John Foreman bringing

Opposite the Minster, the paved area outside St Michael's is the setting for full-immersion baptisms

his own 'kind of inspiration' to the site.

As I leave St Michael's and walk back across the square where once the old belfry stood, the musician in the street greets me with what sounds like the finale of Beethoven's *Choral Symphony*. In my mood of elation, I call out 'thank you' – at which point he loses the tune. As I walk away in embarrassment, the Minster clock chimes the quarters to the metrical psalm tune 'York', once sung on *Songs of Praise* to the words of John Bunyan's hymn, 'He that is down needs fear no fall'. But then someone else heads for St Michael-le-Belfrey, and 'Amazing Grace' begins again. All is forgiven.

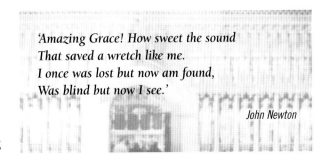

'Amazing Grace! How sweet the sound
That saved a wretch like me.
I once was lost but now am found,
Was blind but now I see.'

John Newton

8
LEEDS
Rainbow People

'A human being is a part of the whole that we call the universe, a part limited in time and space. And yet we experience ourselves, our thoughts and feelings, as something separated from the rest – a kind of optical illusion of our consciousness. This illusion is a prison for us, restricting us to our personal desires and to affection for only the few people nearest us. The task must be to free ourselves from this prison by widening our circle of compassion to embrace all living beings and all of nature.'

Albert Einstein – quoted in the Sunday Bulletin *of All Hallows Church*

Not all the nation's favourite churches are ancient buildings in a beautiful setting. In the rapidly changing city of Leeds lies a small modern building, where hospitality is offered to the stranger, whether casual visitor or desperate refugee.

I have an appointment with a vicar. Ray Gaston should perhaps be called the nation's 'favourite vicar' by the *Songs of Praise* viewer that nominated him. This viewer is one of an invisible band who like to accompany the hymns each week on their own home organ. Although he prefers traditional tunes, he writes that he hopes the nation's favourite churches will include a new inner city church as well as the ancient one at the bottom of the country lane.

I am not sure what my nominated vicar looks like or where he expects me to find him because I have discovered that he has moved to a different church. High above the Kirkstall Road, with its

Ray Gaston, vicar of All Hallows

dense commuter traffic of solitary drivers stop-starting on their daily grind through Leeds, is the very different world of Hyde Park. Here children are playing in streets of Victorian terraced houses teeming with excited voices; the families who live here come from many cultures. And unlike on the metered streets below, there is even space to park, for free! Nearby, above the familiar northern country rooftops, is the large dome and minaret of a mosque. Behind me is a modern yellow-brick building that could be a hall, a café or a church, but which seems to be all three in this instance. People are coming and going, but no one looks like a vicar.

A cyclist has started to pedal very slowly up the steep hill from the main road below. Now, this could be a vicar – healthy, environmentally friendly and fitting exactly the bill for the sort of rector sought in the past. 'The Church of England seeks men of God, grit and gumption,' adding in one parish that 'ideally, he should be a cyclist'.

The hill is so steep that the cyclist, wearing old jeans, is weaving sideways across the road, disappearing out of view before quickly reappearing, but each time advancing only about six feet nearer to me. His progress, if he is the vicar, becomes a sort of *Pilgrim's Progress* on wheels.

I stand and watch as it takes a long time for him to arrive and slowly cycle past me into the church car park. We exchange friendly greetings but he gives no flicker of recognition as he heads for the vicarage. I follow, and the door opens to reveal another man, also wearing worn jeans and a tee shirt. After a brief chat in which I am sort of included, I guess which one is the vicar. But I am only half right. It turns out that they are both vicars. But *the* vicar knows my name.

Parish communion at All Hallows

In Ray Gaston's parish, labels are not worn and not needed. All Hallows is a church where people can come 'who don't feel safe anywhere else'. But it is also a parish that has had more than its fair share of its own problems.

The Parish Church of All Hallows, Hyde Park, Leeds

On the afternoon of 30 April 1970, the then vicar of All Hallows, the Revd Richard Price, looked out of the vicarage window and noticed smoke pouring from his church. By the time darkness fell, the whole of the roof was blazing. Tongues of flames leapt into the evening sky above the church which, for nearly a century, had lived up to a verse from Matthew's Gospel: 'A city set on a hill cannot be hid'. Even as the congregation stood by helpless, watching their much-loved church burn down, a spontaneous collection was being gathered from the huge crowd of onlookers, marking the beginning of the new All Hallows.

The first All Hallows was consecrated on 30 October 1886. For £10,585, the congregation were provided with a large clerestoried nave built of local Potternewton and Meanwood stone, with 'boldly projecting porches' and a square tower 100 feet high 'with fine pinnacles at its south-east corner'.

The Tetley family, brewers and suppliers of the famous tea,

donated the font, the pulpit and the east window featuring 'Our Lord in Glory, enthroned and vested with sceptre and orb'. The altar was given by 300 members of the congregation, each of whom contributed half a crown (twelve and a half pence in today's currency).

Mr Hanson was the first organist, although he had to wait twenty years for the instrument – built by Leeds builders, Abbott and Smith – to be installed. On Whit Monday 1886, the children of the Sunday school were allowed in to the uncompleted building and, clambering over the rafters, became the first to sing in the new church.

In the mid-1970s, when the new All Hallows was under construction, children were kept out for safety reasons, but some things had not changed. As in 1885, there was once again 'an endless succession of teas to raise funds' by what the Victorian vicar had called 'a band of indefatigable workers'. There was one difference however. Without a pulpit in the new church, there could be no repetition of funds being raised with 'vigorous preaching from an insecurely fixed pulpit' on the puzzling text, 'Thou hast found me, O mine enemy'.

The architects of the new All Hallows Church, Peter Brown, Castelow and Partners, created a space that could be set apart for worship but which could also be a gathering place for the surrounding district. The new and much smaller building, completed in 1974, cost £72,050. The steel-framed 'church room' has a tent-like sloping roof of cedar wood above white rough-cast walls. Behind the altar is the only stained glass, a

37

full-length dramatic window on the theme of the four apostles. Canon Price, now retired, will never forget how at first 'the early morning sun spilled through the east window onto the altar, until a new vicarage outside blocked the light'.

In 1999, the building was extended, making space for a community café and drop-in centre, so now people pass in and out of All Hallows throughout the week.

'I'm the only one that's left!' Mrs Brearley is not explaining to me why she is handing out books for the Sunday service in All Hallows (although the person on duty has not turned up), but that she is the only person in the new church who remembers the end of the old building. She told me what happened.

'Everyone was indoors watching TV, even the vicar. And then we saw the smoke.' Rather than being *Songs of Praise*, it was the replay of the

All Hallows Parish

1970 Cup Final between Leeds and Chelsea that had the vicar glued to the screen. The local paper, however, obviously thought this an inappropriate activity for a vicar, and reported that the fire was noticed 'whilst the vicar was discussing church affairs with a group of parishioners'.

Ray Gaston has also appeared in the papers, but for rather more unorthodox behaviour. He was arrested for a sit-down peace protest on the busy Kirkstall Road below the church. He has travelled to Iraq and numbers among his friends many of the Muslims from the nearby mosque, where he has prayed. 'It didn't take me away from Christ, because our true path is to seek Christ and to follow Christ through relationships with people of other faiths', he said in a sermon on the three wise men.

The service in All Hallows begins quietly. There are no formal processions, and only as people arrive do they gather up chairs from around the wall and sit down around the vicar. Ray sits on the floor, distinguished from the congregation only by his white alb. Someone taps a small gong to announce the beginning and end of times of silent prayer and meditation. The sermon on the wedding at Cana is preached by Alison, a young woman who has prepared a table of food for everyone to share as

an illustration of her theme of blessing and hospitality.

Then the whole congregation gathers for communion around the altar, 'the wiggly circle' as Ray calls it. 'If your heart is open to God, then you are welcome.' Children of all ages bring up the bread and the wine for communion, and sit around the altar for the heart of the service. Ray Gaston, who was born in Gloucester, says that as a child he wanted to do 'real church'. In the late 1980s he became an angry atheist, but then he began his journey back to faith before becoming a member of this congregation.

'You really feel you've been to church here,' Ray tells me. I know what he means, and not just because the service lasts almost two hours. There is nothing self-conscious or awkward about the warm welcome given to the stranger. Today this is just me, but the All Hallows family regularly reaches out to help frightened people who have come to the door of this small church in inner city Leeds, refugees from war and torture and seeking asylum. For them, All Hallows is still 'a city set on a hill that cannot be hid'.

Before we go on our separate ways, Andrew asks for volunteers to go with him to visit someone in prison from the Sudan, and Ray announces, 'Good news – Enid's deportation to Uganda has been postponed.' I am beginning to see why the All Hallows newsletter is called *Rainbow People*.

'O God our Creator, in you alone are the riches of life
We come from the East and we come from the West,
Believing we follow, on our different roads,
The same star to the same place.
May we share what we know of its light,
So that we learn from each other the way to the stable,
To worship you our only wealth,
And serve the world with Gospel gold.
Amen.'

Sunday Bulletin *of All Hallows Church*

9
DURHAM
Sanctuary

'*How noble is the deficiency of room for building supplied at Durham, where the Lady Chapel at the west end juts out on an artificial bank of stone and overhangs the precipice which looks down on the Wear! Both Art and Nature have done their utmost to render the burial-place of Venerable Bede in the highest degree sublime.*'

John Mason Neale

The next part of our route retraces St Cuthbert's last journey, a route that will eventually take us across the border into Scotland.

Three hundred years after his death on 20 March 687 on the Farne Islands off the coast of Northumberland, his itinerant monks brought the body of St Cuthbert to his final resting place, the precipice overlooking the River Wear. The story of a dream and a miracle that the monks told was to lead to the building of one of Britain's greatest Norman churches, one in which the remains of both Cuthbert and Bede lie to this day, the latter the most important chronicler of the Dark Ages of British history.

The miracle was claimed as the monks reached the end of their journey in 995, after 300 years of wandering through Northumbria carrying Cuthbert's remains in a shrine,

a wild, dangerous land of robbers and hostile armies. When the shrine was opened, the saint's body was found to be uncorrupted.

The dream was Abbot Eadred's, their leader. He had had the vision in which Cuthbert had visited him saying, 'That my church shall become a safe place of refuge for fugitives, so that any one who flees to my body, for what cause, so ever shall have protection there.'

The dream was honoured for more than 600 years. In the priory around which the cathedral was to be built, watch was kept day and night for refugees. When the Galilee bell rang, the citizens of Durham knew that someone had sought sanctuary in the name of St Cuthbert. Once admitted, the person was given a mattress and food and allowed to attend worship. But reparation for crime went further than mere prayers for forgiveness. A thief had to arrange to pay a fine, and a murderer had thirty-seven days to prepare to leave England forever.

It was 1624, long after the Benedictine priory had been closed by Henry VIII, before sanctuary in the cathedral was finally abolished. By then Scotland and England shared a king, James I, and no longer did invaders cross the border. The successive bishops of Durham did not have royal powers and privileges either any longer, including not

having their own army. But in medieval times Durham, towering high over the precipice with its castle, law courts and the great cathedral, was one of the most powerful places in Britain.

The Cathedral Church of Christ, Blessed Mary the Virgin and St Cuthbert, Durham

The building of the cathedral began in 1092, 100 years after the arrival of St Cuthbert's shrine.

Durham is one of the earliest vaulted cathedrals in Europe and was the very first to use rib vaults. The nave, with its massive cylindrical stone pillars, was built between 1104 and 1128 and the vaulted roof completed in 1135. Canon David Kennedy, precentor of Durham Cathedral today, likens the huge Romanesque pillars to trees with their roots deep in the earth. He thinks that the Norman Bishop Carileph and his architects must have planned a space that inspired worship through its 'robust earthiness' and sense of stability, rather than a fragile beauty. The eye was drawn eastwards to the high altar and the Christ who was in the world rather than upwards to the God of heaven.

Although the eye is still drawn eastwards to the huge rose window lying beyond the altar, this is the thirteenth-century structure and the setting for the chapel of the nine altars. Stripped out in the Reformation, work is now almost complete in restoring these nine separate holy places, with the altar dedicated in 2005 to St Margaret of Scotland, being a sign of peace between two once warring nations.

St Cuthbert, 635–687

It is dark when we enter the cathedral for a pilgrimage that will take our party of Christians from every denomination on a night-time journey from the tomb of the Venerable Bede to the shrine of St Cuthbert. We are an odd mixture of clergy and lay people, full of opinions and gossip about the future of the church, especially of the Church of England that has so often acquired notoriety through its Durham bishops. But our chatter is hushed as we light each other's small candles, the only light to guide our way. The last tourists departed many hours ago, and we are quite alone in the huge space that was designed for Bishop Carileph 900 years ago. The Revd Gilly Myers, the cathedral's succentor, has suggested that we stay quiet and still except when to sing or pray, but it was hardly necessary – the building itself has stilled us.

We began in a much smaller space, the Galilee chapel, where we stood around the simple tomb of Bede, whose history tells us so much about the church 1200 years ago. This monk, said to have learnt almost all that was then to know about language, astronomy and medicine, combined his erudite knowledge to write a vivid history. He wrote that 'the daily charge of singing in church, and the delight of learning and writing, have made up my tranquil life'.

And now we too are 'charged to sing' without the benefit of an organ to keep us in tune, raising our motley voices, both singers and non-singers, in a space that is small enough to separate sheep from goats. There is nothing tranquil in what follows. We are first hesitant and then too loud. We will never be asked to sing on *Songs of Praise*.

In single file we make our pilgrimage down the long nave, used in the English Civil War as a prison, but for centuries before as the beginning of freedom as fugitives claimed sanctuary. It seems a long way, guided only by our tiny guttering candles, and we walk silently, each alone with our own thoughts. Then something strange happens. Near the high altar, the way through the dark becomes so difficult that we begin helping one another to avoid stumbling. Only a minute or two later, when stopping around the stone set in the floor inscribed with the single word 'Cuthbertus' in order to sing, we have evolved from a crowd into a choir.

*'Glory to thee, my God, this night
For all the blessings of the light;
Keep me, O keep me, King of kings,
Beneath thy own almighty wings.
Forgive me, Lord, for thy dear Son,
The ill that I this day have done,
That with the world, myself and thee,
I, ere I sleep, at peace may be.'*

Tonight in his cathedral, it feels as though we have all claimed the sanctuary of Cuthbert, saint and healer, and that the God whom he loved has forgiven us.

*'Praise God from whom all blessings flow,
Praise him all creatures here below,
Praise him above, ye heavenly host,
Praise Father, Son, and Holy Ghost.'*

Thomas Ken

10

USHAW

Coming Back to the Heart of Worship

*'**T**he following decree was proposed by Barrere and adopted:*

Art 1: The National Convention denounces the British Government to Europe and the English nation.

Art 2: Every Frenchman that shall place his money in the English funds, shall be declared a traitor to his country.

Art 4: All foreigners, subjects of the powers now at war with France, particularly the English, shall be arrested, and seals put upon their papers.

Art 6: All good citizens shall be bound in the name of the country, to search for the foreigners who are concerned in the plot denounced.

Art 13: Marie Antoinette shall be delivered over to the revolutionary tribunal, and shall immediately be conducted to the prison of the Conciergerie.'

from the proceedings of the (Revolutionary) National Convention, Paris 18 July 1793 – The Scots Magazine, Edinburgh, printed by Murray and Cochrane 1793

A short walk from the city boundary up into the hills above Durham stands Ushaw College, its Roman Catholic chapel designed by one of the most gifted, albeit eccentric, Victorian architects, Augustus Welby Northmore Pugin. The story of the college began in 1793 when the French Revolution was at its height.

A small group of English Roman Catholics were in the seminary at Douai preparing for ordination when England declared war on the Republic and life in anti-religious revolutionary France suddenly became doubly dangerous for the young men. They were imprisoned within the country, in fear of their lives, but continued to pray and study together, even improvising an altar through draping a white sheet over a discarded window frame, balanced on a bread basket. They were eventually able to escape across to England, helped by shadowy figures that may well have acted as the inspiration for Baroness Orczy's fictional League of the Scarlet Pimpernel, although the young seminarians' destination was not to be the luxurious homes of the English aristocracy.

One of the Douai students described their arrival on the chilly moors of County Durham, where just four miles west and in sight of Durham's Anglican Cathedral, they were to become the first of many thousands of priests to be trained at Ushaw. 'After escaping Egyptian slavery, we arrived safely at the land of promise; at the same time, I wish I could say it flowed with milk and honey.' Their new home was short on 'milk and honey', but their superiors appreciated the 'cheapness of fuel and provisions' (Ushaw Seminary later even had its own coalmine and gas works), and it was thought that impressionable young men should prepare for their vocation under a regime of disciplined isolation. Many of the older generation of Catholic priests living today who were trained at Ushaw still remember this strict seclusion away from their families for as long as three years.

Nowadays, with an easy drive from Durham, visitors are welcome at Ushaw and its huge and sumptuously decorated Victorian chapel dedicated to St Cuthbert.

Augustus Welby Northmore Pugin, 1812–1852

St Cuthbert's Chapel, Ushaw College, Durham

St Cuthbert's Chapel was designed by Augustus Welby Northmore Pugin. Born in 1812, he was a tortured genius with a passionate desire to recreate the lost spirit of the age of medievalism and designed many churches in such a mood. But his life was as tragic as it was short, with his first wife dying in childbirth followed by his second also, in 1844, the year that the building of the Ushaw Seminary Chapel began. By 1851 his imagination had began to overheat and he seemed to have lost his mind. His behaviour then became so eccentric that his third wife had him confined to a lunatic asylum. A year later, just two days after his release, he had a stroke and died. He was forty.

Pugin's father came from a French Protestant family, and had left France after the Revolution, but he took his son on many trips back to visit the great Gothic Catholic cathedrals, including Chartres. These visits affected the faith of Pugin so strongly that he converted to Roman Catholicism. But he was appalled by the Classical Revival in England, which he saw as pagan. The plain utilitarian boxes with their pedimented porticos, such as St John's, Waterloo Road in London, built after the final defeat of Napoleon in 1815, were anathema to him.

'I gained my faith', he wrote, 'beneath the vaulted roofs of Lincoln Cathedral and Westminster Abbey.'

Pugin was a difficult man, impatient with clients but reserving his greatest venom for ecclesiastical committees and accountants. His designs were ornate and highly decorated, but the money usually ran out long before his vision was completed. He was always intensely dissatisfied with the results, and once described the painted decoration of one of his own designs as looking as if it had 'been produced by a troop of beetles crawling through a paint pot and then up the plaster'. He also decried the lack of fonts in many churches, 'a jug and basin, much as might be used by puritans and fanatics, are the only substitute, and these in places where silver tea services are being subscribed for the clergyman!'

With Ushaw, a furious battle erupted between church leaders and college authorities about Pugin's designs, which were out of keeping with the rest of the Georgian buildings. One Catholic bishop demanded a building that would resemble St Peter's in Rome. Work on the chapel finally began, however, in 1844 and was completed in 1848, but without the lofty spire that the architect had specified. It was described as 'superior to all the chapels of the ancient universities, except King's College, Cambridge', and its services were 'the best conducted anywhere in England'.

Today, entering the huge chapel with its collegiate-style seating facing inward, where once 400 students worshipped, we are in a Gothic Revival building that was once described as 'pure Pugin, from foundation to roof'. But this isn't quite true, as Pugin's original design in all its ornate splendour was found to be too small and provided too little seating for the students and too much for their teachers. In 1882, the architectural practice of Dunn and Hansom began the intricate task of dismantling Pugin's work and preserving all the materials for reuse in a much larger building, while retaining the spirit of the original design.

The present west window was once at the east end above the high altar, and the English decorated style of Pugin's choir

'Virgin and Child' by Karl Hoffmann

was replaced by a French Gothic form. The new architects tried to emulate Pugin's style in the exotic three-sided apse, with its gables and pinnacles above the high altar. The whole structure, costing £14,430, was blessed on 4 October 1884, although the chapel was not consecrated until 1897, when all the bills had finally been paid by Ushaw's benefactors and subscribers.

Not for the first time, I got lost trying to find one of the nation's favourite churches. There is an easy route from Durham City to Ushaw, but I wanted to photograph the chapel and its surroundings from a nearby hilltop. A lot of time, however, was wasted discovering that there isn't such a view, since Ushaw's buildings lie in an almost secret seclusion; perhaps this is not surprising since, in its early days, anti-Catholic protesters roamed around the area intent on causing trouble.

By late afternoon, I had finally caught a glimpse of a few Victorian buildings at the end of a long drive. A narrow entrance through a high wall led into dark and gloomy woods; it felt as if no one had passed this way for years. As my car bounced along the track, the building reappeared, complete with a vast chapel. Crows flapped and swooped over the turrets and spires, and I heard an owl hooting. Wooden baulks were nailed across the entrance and a notice warned visitors to 'keep out – dangerous structure!' A pigeon flew out of one of the tall

windows. The double-fronted doors seemed permanently barred against admission and for a few moments I felt as though I was caught up in a Gothic horror story. Already late for an ecumenical conference at the college, a place that I had heard so much about but never seen, irrational fears started to take over. What had happened to my friends, and where were they behind all these decidedly sinister windows and arches?

I drove on, and eventually found the main college buildings further down the track, and with the conference already well underway. I later learned from one of the college staff, Father Gillespie, that the ruins which had so spooked me had once been the junior seminary, designed by Pugin's son. Here small boys had boarded, living as austerely as the seminarians. Once a week they had been allowed to socialize with the older students, and were able to visit the main buildings through a passage, nicknamed 'the crying corridor', because it was so often the setting for tears when time was up to return to junior school. One small boy who had been sent to this school for a time until, much to his relief, he became ill and was sent home never to return, grew up to be the Shakespearean actor and Hollywood star, Ian Bannen.

Father Gillespie told me that he thought the old building could have been the original inspiration for Hogwarts Wizards' Academy in the *Harry Potter* stories, and then quickly went on to make another connection with them, explaining the purpose behind a huge range of battlements surrounding a field in the grounds, also designed by Pugin. In the days when 400 students lived at Ushaw, they played a strange game called 'Cat'. One player bounced a ball three times, and his opponent had to hit it on the third bounce with a huge bat, before running round the battlements. Could the game of 'Quidditch', so favoured by Harry Potter, have evolved from this?

Although the Chapel of St Cuthbert is open to all, Ushaw has many long dark corridors and with less than thirty students living here today, it is a welcome sight to find another human quietly padding through a cloister, ready to help lost visitors find the chapel.

Father Gillespie had told me that it was easy, 'just walk to the red wall and turn right.' In a spare moment (but allowing at least thirty minutes), I unravelled a metaphorical ball of string, found the red wall and hurried down cloisters and corridors lined with oil paintings of both past students and saints. Eventually I came to a locked door that, according to my instructions, should have been the entrance to the chapel. Then I sensed something behind me. Turning round, it was there, the great chapel, open and filled with sunlight and welcoming me in.

The first thing to catch the eye is Pugin's huge lectern in the centre. In its day, it was a work of cutting-edge design and one of England's contributions to the Arts and Industries of All Nations exhibited at the Great Exhibition of 1851. There is also a statue of the Virgin and Child in the antechapel, carved from a single piece of marble by Karl Hoffmann, a Jew who converted to Roman Catholicism in the 1850s. When the sun comes out, you can make out a tiny Star of David engraved on Mary's clothing. The chapel itself is richly decorated, a place to stand and stare at and absorb slowly. It is also somehow the most welcoming place within the college, and seems to bring one to the heart of things.

All our conference participants came together for worship at the end of a day during which we had discussed Christian worship on TV and *Songs of Praise* in particular. The chapel was filled with warm evening sunlight filtering through the immense stained glass windows when we began our prayers, and even though we were a tiny group, with some having to be rescued by a search party, we did not feel lost sitting on the polished wooden benches, where once hundreds of students assembled several times each day. I hoped that I might be sitting in the place where Cardinal Heenan had sat when he began his training here.

We had a musician with us, and he filled the building with French music taken from Pugin's time, playing the chapel's Bishop organ that had been built in 1847. As a group, however, we were not confident enough to attempt plainsong, the subject of a booklet written in 1850 by Pugin in an attempt to rekindle the medieval spirit within worship. But 'an earnest appeal for the revival of the ancient plain song' has encouraged Father Gillespie to play and sell plainchant CDs in his college bookshop.

We used as our reading a part of a song by Matt Redman:

'When the music fades, all is stripped away,
And I simply come;
Longing just to bring something that's of worth
That will bless your heart.
I'll bring You more than a song,
For a song in itself
Is not what you have required.
You search much deeper within
Through the way things appear;
You're looking into my heart.
I'm coming back to the heart of worship,
And it's all about You,
All about You, Jesus.
I'm sorry, Lord, for the thing I've made it,
When it's all about You,
All about You, Jesus.'

Matt Redman

Extract from the song 'When the Music Fades' by Matt Redman.
Copyright © 1997 Kingsway Music

For all its seclusion, elaborate architecture and strange history, Pugin's chapel at Ushaw had indeed brought us back to the heart of worship and the next day I travelled on in the steps of St Cuthbert, listening to the ancient chants that the saint would have both known and sung.

11

CORSENSIDE
No Man's Land

'*As I go on I feel that every bend of the road will bring me face to face with the Promised Land. A wilderness cannot continue forever. In the desert you can smell the oasis long before its palm trees break the skyline. So it seems to me as I mount hills and descend into valleys, cross streams and skirt the shoulders of hills, that I can feel Scotland round the next corner. But how wrong I am! The Border – that No Man's Land between England and Scotland – is a wide and persistent wilderness. It has a spirit of its own.*

This side of Hadrian's Wall was never tamed. It has made many songs but no laws.'

From In Search of Scotland *by H.V. Morton*

Far from the immense pillars of Durham, almost at the border with Scotland, a remote church, hardly bigger than a cottage, was one of St Cuthbert's resting places.

It's a place also that brings me back to childhood.

As a child, I spent many winter Sunday afternoons reading H.V. Morton, in a book my father kept almost as a sacred relic in the glass-fronted cupboard where the special ones were kept. Just to unlock the door and catch the smell of old volumes was to begin a journey into Scotland. Morton's book chimed with my father's stories of driving across the border and seeing ghostly Roman legions on the march. As I read about the wild road north, the aching boredom of a Sunday afternoon spent in dull suburban London was immediately forgotten, replaced by longing for a faraway promised land.

Then each summer, the dream would come true, as we drove the same road that H.V. Morton had described, up to Carter Bar. When we finally reached the border

with Scotland, my father would jump out of the family Ford Consul, and reappear as a Pictish customs officer to demand our passports. A good friend recently revealed that his father did exactly the same, and we agreed that the real reason for the pause was probably for a much-needed cigarette.

It remains today a very long and solitary leg on travels home to Scotland. Looking at the log that I used to keep as a boy to while away the miles, there was nothing to record in my *Eye-Spy Book of the Road*. Fifty years on, for most people the journey up the A68 from the last substantial English village to Carter Bar is not a second faster. But for me now, it has become much slower, ever since one gloomy evening, just as the car topped the long hill out of West Woodburn, a shaft of sunlight picked out a tiny church across the moor. For those who like their favourite churches to be hidden away from the crowds, here was a real gem.

The Old Church of Corsenside St Cuthbert, West Woodburn

There is a legend that sometime between 875 and 995, monks who for over 300 years cared for the body of Cuthbert, concealing his shrine whenever they could, came to this hillside north of the modern village of West Woodburn, and built a small two cell church to shelter his coffin.

Later a medieval village developed around a twelfth-century church, which was not altered until the seventeenth century, when a priest door was inserted in the south wall. A century later, a bell cote was added and in 1741, a bell was presented so that the vicar, David Gordon, could summon the faithful.

The medieval village was abandoned around 1750, when

the first bridge was built across the River Rede, at the bottom of the valley, to carry traffic from London to Edinburgh. Today's bridge and the road are both part of a network that was built following the defeat of the Jacobite Bonnie Prince Charlie at Culloden, to help move troops more easily. It made use of Dere Street, a Roman road, built for the same purpose at a time when Hadrian's Wall was thought to mark the edge of the civilized world.

Although the old church of Corsenside was already slumbering, in the nineteenth century a small chancel was added at the east end. Today, except for the summer Sunday once a year when Christians walk up from West Woodburn for a communion service and a picnic, St Cuthbert's Church waits for the inquisitive passer-by.

The notice 'twelfth-century church' is so small, and the entrance along a rutted track that leads to a closed farm gate so unobtrusive, that I begin to think that I have made a mistake and driven accidentally into a field of cattle. But bouncing on past the wall of a farmhouse, Cuthbert's bell cote comes into view, and just in front of it another little gate leading into a large graveyard. Having sung the song 'John Brown's body lies a mouldering in his grave' years ago at school, I never expected to find it! But it is here – or at least his namesake. Another grave is freshly dug just below the church, highlighting clearly that ancestors still return here to rest in peace on a beautiful Northumbrian hillside.

Except for the sound of the wind scudding across the upland fields, it is quiet. A village lies buried here, one that vanished 250 years ago.

The church door opens easily to visitors but according to a cartoon pinned to the door showing a cheerful cow lifting the latch, equally easily to cattle and sheep. I remember on one occasion walking up to the door of a similar church while filming the hymn writer, Sydney Carter, and the writer, Malcolm Muggeridge. They arrived having somehow acquired a large flock of curious sheep, eager to join them inside.

The cartoon turns my mind from thinking about Corsenside as a centre of heavenly rest into more of a place of heavenly birth. Inside it is simple and primitive. With its bare stone walls and floor, it could be a byre, where cows might have once joined sheep and their shepherds around a manger. In a tiny Victorian chancel, simple wooden rails protect the altar around which Christians must have gathered for centuries to hear the story of angels and wise men. The Bible is still open, and the atmosphere is as holy as it is homely. I can easily believe that 1,000 years ago, in dark and dangerous days, the body of a saint was sheltered here. My spiritual batteries are newly charged, ready for the drive north into H.V. Morton's 'wide and persistent wilderness'.

'Gracious Lord, we thank you for your servant Cuthbert, in life a minister of your grace, in death a channel of your glory. Grant that in the glad company of your saints we may journey on in faith, and at last be brought home to your dwelling place in joy; through our Lord and Saviour Jesus Christ.
Amen.'

12

HADDINGTON
'The Lamp of Lothian'

*'**T**he Estates of Parliament now convened having considered the depositions of Agnes Hunter, Margaret Dickson, and Isobell Murray, taken by the Ministers and Magistrates and Elders of that Congregation by the which they confess sundrie points of the crime of witchcraft… and the Estates of Parliament being desirous to clear the land of wickedness… if they be found guilty of the said Crime of Witchcraft, to convict and condemne them and give furth the sentence of death against them cause strangle them and burn their bodies to death.'*

Commission from the Scots Parliament meeting on 23 May 1649, sent to the minister and elders of St Mary's Haddington

St Mary's Haddington, much of which had been wrecked in the sixteenth century by English invaders, has been a regular venue for *Songs of Praise* since 1973 when the church was restored to its full grandeur. It is the first Presbyterian church to contain an Episcopalian chapel. But there have also been dark moments in its history.

When Daniel Defoe came to Haddington early in the eighteenth century, he would have found the parish church looking very similar to how I first saw it in the late 1960s. It seems also that he probably felt much as I did. 'Tis easy to see that it is not like what it has been,' he wrote. 'There are some monuments of the Maitlands, antient lords of this part of the country remaining; but as the choir of the church is open and defac'd, the monuments of the dead have suffer'd with the rest.'

In April 1548, Haddington was caught in the conflict between England and Scotland as an English army, including the Bishop of Durham's own troops, seized it. But it was the combined French and Scottish artillery besieging it that finally put pay to the choir and transepts

'The Crucifixion with the Virgin and St John' by Edward Burne-Jones, 1877

of the church as well as much of the rest of the town. In fact, by the time it had been 'dung doon with great ordnance', the English occupiers had caught the plague, and many made their escape on 19 September 1549, looting as much as they could carry, including the church bells.

Before he died in 1573, the great reformer John Knox, who may have been born near to the church in 1505, ordered a wall to be built to enclose the surviving west end of the nave so that the church could be used again. This was to be the home of the same congregation that took part in the search for and persecution of women accused of witchcraft during the seventeenth century.

In 1811, the nave was restored again with pews to accommodate 1,233 people facing Knox's wall against which, from 1893, stood the organ. But this wall, that had in the 1960s helped form the impression of a dark and stuffy Kirk for such an elegant county town as East Lothian, was totally transformed in the summer of 1973, when it was demolished and one of the finest interiors of any church in Scotland was revealed once more.

The Collegiate Church of St Mary's, Haddington

A few years after the death of Francis of Assisi in 1226, Franciscan Grey Friars came to Haddington and built what was described as 'a church of wonderful beauty' on the banks of the River Tyne. The choir of their church was so admired for its elegance and its light interior that it became known as Lucerna Laudoniae – the Lamp of Lothian. This building was destroyed in 1356.

Shortly after that, a few hundred yards to the south, Scotland's largest parish church was built from local red sandstone in a decorated style with some Norman features. This building is 197 feet long with a nave and choir of equal length. The tower, which since 1999 has contained a ring of eight bells replacing the ones stolen in 1548, was originally crowned with a lantern steeple similar to St Giles' Cathedral in Edinburgh. The remaining tower is still referred to as 'the Lamp of Lothian' and is a prominent landmark for travellers.

In the seventeenth century, the ruined sacristy was repaired and became a burial place for the Maitland family. This Lauderdale Aisle has since been transformed into an ecumenical place of prayer, and a focus for the annual Haddington pilgrimage. A scallop shell in the nave is a reminder of the medieval pilgrimages from Haddington to Compostela in Spain.

When the choir was re-roofed in 1973, fibreglass was used for the vaulting, but it looks exactly like stone. A fine, visually stunning, modern organ built by a local builder dominates the north transept. There is much late Victorian stained glass, some by Burne-Jones including one given in 1973 by the Victoria and Albert Museum, which was originally in a church in Torquay. Amazingly, this large window fitted exactly into the existing stone tracery.

After thirty years of worshipping in the darker end of the church but looking through to the brighter but less-used restored choir, the congregation have now migrated east into the light.

On a winter Sunday, the Revd Jim Cowie is preparing for a family service in St Mary's. It will begin with an announcement in formal language that would not have seemed out of place in the sixteenth century, and describes the proposal to ordain Sara Macgill as an Elder. This is a lifelong responsibility although she will not, unlike her Presbyterian predecessors, have to administer justice to witches.

The man in the bright blue pullover in the praise band, tuning his electric guitar, is a former Chief Inspector of Constabulary for Scotland. Sir Roy Cameron is a far from stern session clerk and admits to being a slow learner as a musician. His 'enquiries' this morning extend only to the search for the 'Christmas cake address list', by which the housebound people of Haddington will get a seasonal present from the congregation.

Before a sizeable congregation of all ages arrives, the minister of St Mary's has helped complete a technical rig almost as complex as that needed for *Songs of Praise*. Sara Macgill and her husband John, a journalist, unravel a spaghetti-like mass of cables. Sara operates the PowerPoint presentation that highlights images and Bible texts as well as displaying the hymn words which, this week, are taken from the *Songs of Praise* Top Twenty. Jim Cowie reminds the congregation as the service starts that after all twenty have been sung, they are to vote for their own favourites. 'Peter, our choir director, and I want you to become a real singing congregation.' It is clear that in spite of many appearances on *Songs of Praise*, more is to be expected.

As we stand to sing 'Praise my soul the King of heaven', three small boys brandishing collecting bowls are bouncing rhythmically in time to the tune. But before they take up the collection with much gravitas, we all have to participate in something else. The story from Mark's Gospel of John the Baptist on the banks of the Jordan is displayed with key words missing. Everyone is encouraged to call out the missing words. 'River Jordan!' 'Locusts!' 'Wild bees – no, no, wild honey!' we all yell.

What follows, a sermon and prayers, is made effective through the minister's relaxed style. I learn from one of the congregation, however, that behind the informality is the same intense preparation that Presbyterian ministers have always put into the traditional sermon. 'Jim does not sleep on Saturday night.'

I confess to being a bit traditional, used to a fifteen-minute sermon delivered by an orator. But Jim is quickly winning me over, even to the idea – once anathema – of singing with the hymn words displayed on the screen. Somehow, we are beginning to be a singing congregation and not just muttering into our individual hymnbooks as usual. I am surprising myself.

Surrounded by all his high-tech equipment, I might once have thought that parish ministers like Jim Cowie were hoping to emulate the world of the TV evangelist.

But today he appears as vulnerable as the rest of us in the middle of his praise band. Sharing worship rather than leading it, we are learning something new together. Suddenly a single sentence from the Bible gains a new significance.

'It's not a straight path to the Promised Land,' says Jim, reflecting on a verse from the book of Joshua. 'It is full of danger and doubts.' This feels like an honest admission from a minister who, as convenor of one of the Church of Scotland's most important boards,

responsible for social work and the care of the elderly at
a time of dwindling funds, certainly knows all about
dangers and doubts.

The old ghosts of orators denouncing the world from
the pulpit, condemning the sinner and even burning the
occasional witch, evaporate in the warm light of this new
space. Out of its violent past the Lamp of Lothian, first
restored by Knox, is now 'a singular solace', open to all,
a place of reconciliation and pilgrimage.

What I have been given this morning in St Mary's is
a light to pick up and carry forward on my own spiritual
journey.

'This is a house of prayer: may God be known to
you here.
This is the home of Christ's people: may you find
His welcoming here.
Heaven and Earth are met in this place.
May the sense of that lighten your burdens,
quieten your fears, encourage your faith
and then send you home to serve Him well,
and make His Church a praise to His name.'

A prayer offered for each visitor to St Mary's Haddington

13

OBAN, ARGYLL AND BUTE

Love Behind the Billows

'*We now left those illustrious ruins, by which Mr Boswell was much affected, nor would I willingly be thought to have looked upon them without some emotion. Perhaps in the revolutions of the world, Iona may be sometime again the instructress of the world... We had a good day and a fine passage, and in the evening landed at Oban, where we found a tolerable inn.*'

from Johnson and Boswell in Scotland, *first published 1773*

More than 1,400 years ago, men stood on the shore of a small island off the west coast of Scotland and watched as a boat, made from leather and containing thirteen strangers, was beached. They were immediately wary, for although the sea was the highway of the time for law-abiding people, raiders and illegal traders also travelled the same route. But this boat carried a man called Columba and twelve of his companions. The Christian gospel they were bringing to the island of Iona was to spread from the abbey which they had founded for the rest of Scotland.

The cathedral named after St Columba overlooks a bay where today thousands of pilgrims set sail for Iona in search of Celtic spirituality, and where, in less happy times, exiled Scots took a last glimpse of their homeland. For the long centuries in Scotland since the saint's arrival have been marked by cruelty and violence. In 1746, the Catholic pretender to the throne, Charles Edward Stewart Bonnie, was pursued to these Atlantic shores after his army was defeated at Culloden, and the people of Highland Scotland were persecuted and deprived of their Gaelic culture; early in the nineteenth century, landowners began the 'clearances', ethnically cleansing the land of the traditional crofters in order to replace them with flocks of sheep.

But the gospel brought to Scotland by St Columba survived, and when in 1878 Roman Catholic bishops were restored to Scotland, Angus MacDonald, a priest from the West Highlands, became the first Bishop of Argyll and the Isles. He set about building his cathedral on a site overlooking Oban Bay.

The Roman Catholic Cathedral of St Columba, Oban

Although the bishop had the good fortune to possess a prime site, the funds available for a building could stretch no further than for a corrugated-iron building. All agreed that when the 'Tin Cathedral', as it was known, opened in 1886, it was a 'make-do' arrangement; it was a 'make-do', however, that had to last for over fifty years.

By 1932, enough money had been raised, mainly in Canada, America and Ireland by descendants of the Scots who had been exiled in the clearances, to begin construction of a new cathedral in traditional granite. The architect was Sir Giles Gilbert Scott, world-famous designer of the red telephone box, who was also responsible for another of the nation's favourites, Liverpool's Anglican Cathedral. For Sir Giles, Oban was a modest design in his trademark style, neo-Gothic. The simple, open interior makes use of natural light and even at dusk is not gloomy. The tower, in what is the largest church building in the Highlands, provides a sturdy landmark, welcoming the seafarer to the safe haven of Oban's natural harbour.

St Columba's Cathedral was finally completed in 1959, when two huge bells named Brendan and Kenneth were hung in the tower.

Songs of Praise has visited the cathedral at least three times. The building has a resonant acoustic, rare in Scotland, and I still remember the mystical sound in the 1973 programme when a large choir of young people sang hymns in Gaelic. But until now, my experience of this cathedral had been entirely through the medium of television. Visiting a church seen on *Songs of Praise* can sometimes be a disappointment; once the television lamps tinting the walls with colour and creating light and shadow have gone, the empty building can seem dour and drab. Not so here.

The doors of St Columba's are still open as the sun goes down, but the building glows through the evening light, the legacy of an architect who knew how to do it.

young backpackers talking in many different accents and languages photograph a tranquil scene. A Russian cruise liner is tied up at the Railway Pier below and the sea is almost flat calm. The world seems at peace with itself.

Celtic Christianity came to Scotland with St Columba in the seventh century, but the people that have kept the faith since then have endured terrible onslaughts. Sometimes their adversary was the invader, sometimes a fickle and hostile climate which could turn a journey at sea into a dangerous duel with nature. Always, though, they saw God in everything.

At the beginning of the twentieth century, Alexander Carmichael, born close to Oban on the island of Lismore and by profession a civil servant, began to collect Celtic prayers. One of these prayers he heard said in earnest by a seafarer preparing for a journey by night by the light of the moon. It became our prayer as in the gathering darkness over the sea, which some believe St Brendan crossed to reach America, we watched a tiny boat leave harbour.

It does not seem empty either because of a feature that we first experienced in a Catholic church in France. My wife Liz had been there to pray, and reported how she had been supported by some monks chanting behind the vestry door. She wondered why they had locked themselves in. When we both later visited the French church together, singing could be heard once again, but the note-perfect choir was in fact coming from a strategically hidden tape. This arrangement is also being used, to the same effect, in Oban, where a tape is playing so quietly that I feel I am listening to St Columba and his monks singing in the huge West Highland sky above the cathedral.

Later, as I climb up the hill above Oban, the sun is sinking behind distant mountains and the lifeboat returns to port, passing the reassuring silhouette of the cathedral named after the saint who travelled across dangerous waters to bring Christianity to Scotland. Around me,

'Glory be to Thee O God of Life,
for the guiding lamp of ocean.
Be Thine own hand
on my rudder's helm,
and Thy love
behind the billows.'

from Celtic Prayers *selected by Avery Brooke from the collection of Alexander Carmichael*

14
BELFAST
Saints in Cregagh

'*Stones are easy to throw and few can afford to throw them.'*

From a sermon on Radio 4 preached by Noel Battye, rector of Cregagh

The sixth-century Celtic saints, Columba and Finnian, used the sea crossing between Scotland and Ireland as we would today use a motorway. Then the gospel that they carried travelled at the speed of their oarsmen, but today modern broadcasting carries stories of faith between the two countries in a microsecond.

The first ever *Songs of Praise* from Northern Ireland was broadcast just a month after the series itself began, on 1 October 1961. It came from Malone Presbyterian Church in Belfast's Lisburn Road, and was introduced by Edgar 'Billy' Boucher, who went on to present many programmes from the Province over the next fifteen years. I was making my first visit to the city around that time also. Arriving into the Edwardian splendour of the old Great Victoria Street Station, I was grilled by a customs officer who gravely inspected my battered camera and asked if I was smuggling it in from the Republic of Ireland.

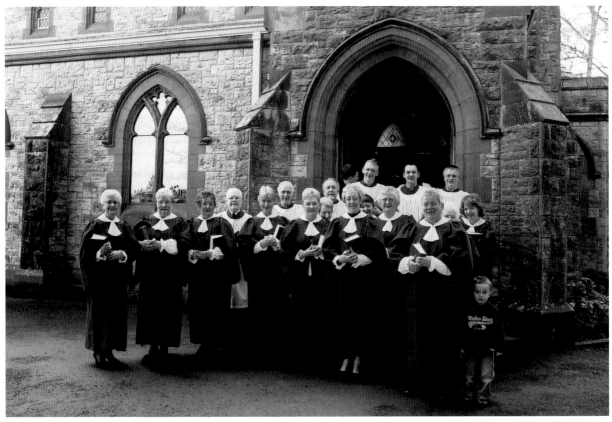

The choir of St Finnian's Parish Church

towns and beautiful countryside of the Province, 3,000 people would lose their lives in the three decades following *Songs of Praise*'s and my first visit. Amongst the casualties were two BBC engineers killed by a landmine in 1971, with many other film crews also hurt, caught in the midst of crossfire. Belfast had become an eerie place.

Songs of Praise broadcasts continued to come from Northern Ireland throughout those dark days, but tried to tell a different story. As real as all the news footage of bombings and shootings were, the images *Songs of Praise* showed, taken from everyday life, were of generous hospitality and deep faith, showing how the majority of Catholics and Protestants were praying, singing and working together for peace. The series began to include interviews with local people in 1977, and this 'alternative' viewpoint formed an important part of the story of Northern Ireland.

In 2005, *Songs of Praise* from St Anne's Cathedral showed a city determined to look forwards, not back. Although everyone living in Belfast had been affected by the events of those terrible years, it is not what they want to talk about now.

Belfast was experiencing an autumn monsoon and I spent my visit on the city's trolleybuses whooshing through flooded streets. It was long before I knew about *Songs of Praise* and my goal was not to visit a church but instead the Belfast Transport Museum, but I ended up horribly lost. As I now know, after many return visits to this most hospitable of cities, everyone always wants to help. With complete confidence, everyone that I asked each suggested an entirely different location where they insisted I 'could not miss it'. I went backwards and forwards through the city streets until finally, coming to a side street of neat terraced houses dimly lit by elegant Victorian gas lamps, I gave up.

I barely noticed that the kerb stones in that particular street were painted red, white and blue, and felt only mild interest when the train from Dublin crept gingerly across a rickety bridge where the IRA had detonated a bomb just the day before.

I saw the same streets making headlines in the television news some ten years later. They formed the front line in a sectarian conflict where neighbours had become enemies. Here, along with the surrounding

The Church of Ireland Parish Church of St Finnian's, Cregagh, County Down

In 1932, 1,500 years after St Patrick arrived in Ireland, the BBC opened a new radio drama studio in Belfast. And in south Belfast, in fields where dairy cows had once grazed, providing the city's milk, a new church was built to serve a growing residential district. While the church records speak of the many people that helped 'create a communion of saints in Cregagh', it largely came about through the vision of a local curate, Mr Huston. Land had to be found and then purchased, and £12,000 had to be raised not just for a building but to pay for clergy. It was a fundraising effort involving many people, and with the leadership and persistence of Mr Huston the foundation stone was laid in 1931, 'on probably the finest site occupied by any church in Belfast'.

St Finnian's, Cregagh was consecrated on 10 September

1932. The building was designed by a local architect, W. Taggart, in an early English style using stone from a nearby quarry at Scrabo. It is about 100 feet long, and on each side of a spacious nave are columns and arches of reconstituted Bath stone. At the west end is an octagonal baptistery of white Giffnock stone containing the font. An unusual innovation at the time was the use of concealed electric lighting throughout the church.

Over the years, right up to a recent addition in the north aisle, brilliantly-coloured stained glass has been installed.

Noel Battye, the third rector of St Finnian's, begins his day while most of us are still asleep. But this Sunday his early start has an extra purpose. He is hoping to persuade 500 parishioners that they should all rise an hour early for Lent. While Belfast slumbers, he is up worrying away at a sermon in which he will suggest that an extra hour awake provides time for a daily 'BANJO'! (Bang a nasty job off!). For a man whose preaching has made him a popular broadcaster, it is a surprise to discover that every sermon he prepares is Noel's personal BANJO! He faces

his fears head on as he reads and rereads his text, as dawn breaks over Belfast.

It was around dawn when Noel Battye and I used to meet for *This is the Day*, the BBC religious service that for ten years went out 'live' on BBC1 at 9.30 every Sunday morning. Noel was an ideal presenter, since rehearsals had to begin by 7 a.m. and everything took place in a viewer's home besieged by cameramen and engineers. He was the one person who always appeared fully functioning at these ungodly hours, and would make himself immediately at home in strange surroundings.

I have never forgotten the way that Noel could sit and talk cheerfully to a family he had met only minutes before, putting them at ease as their house filled up with yawning people carrying cameras, microphones, lights and other broadcasting paraphernalia. He was a centre of stillness, while others were hurrying in and out, and I was tearing my hair out with worry about all the things that could go wrong in a live broadcast.

I discovered part of his secret when I visited his parish recently: Noel spends a great deal of time each day visiting his parishioners. Sometimes they are in hospital or prison, and for a while he was a chaplain at Crumlin Road Prison, but mostly his days are spent in people's living rooms, just as he did for *This is the Day*. Noel says, 'What use am I to this church if I am not listening to my parishioners?'

On Sunday's in St Finnian's, there are four services, all well attended, and as one congregation departs another surges in. This Sunday there is also to be a special party for older residents, and between all this Noel will slip in his regular 'live' one-hour broadcast, *Sounds Sacred*, for BBC Radio Ulster, of which he is presenter, producer and engineer. Then there is a meal to be cooked for his young and energetic curate, Aonghus, as well as any extra visits to parishioners that can be fitted in.

Both Noel's churchwardens are in their early twenties, and two young women lead prayers. Halfway through a service, Noel suddenly remembers some good news: the parish is one of five in County Down putting together a team of builders to spend their holidays in Uganda constructing new schools; the latest school had been expected to attract 100 children, but on the opening day 330 enrolled for classes.

Noel's preaching can also turn surprising corners, especially when he turns to the subject of religion. 'It is too easy to sit in judgment on people, putting them in boxes, for having attitudes to others that are simply wrong in the sight of God. This is not, not, *not* about "them", it's about us – all of us – you and me. We must be brutally honest with ourselves; these are sins that go along with being religious.'

Neither the congregation of St Finnian's nor its rector fits into any box, even though in so many ways the worship is traditional and the parish is wonderfully normal. In spite of the history of violence all around, here – as *Songs of Praise* has witnessed – the centre holds and familiar things survive.

Others with needs live in the rectory. Harriet is in remission from cancer, Giles is a refugee and Finn is recovering from a broken leg. Meet the rectory dogs. Harriet, a little spaniel who was abused by a previous owner and Giles, a large black Heinz 57 dog who, when accused of biting someone, sought the sanctuary of the church, have been joined by Finn (Finnian), a young red setter who has yet to learn that traffic is dangerous.

Late at night, Finn leads the rector on a boisterous circuit around the church grounds. The church is floodlit and the youth club still in full swing. Belfast, laid out in the distance below, looks to be at peace. Tomorrow Noel will be down amongst its streets to see how true that is. 'God is patient with us,' says Noel, 'so long as we make a start.'

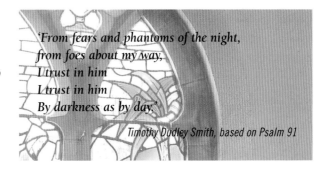

'From fears and phantoms of the night,
from foes about my way,
I trust in him
I trust in him
By darkness as by day.'

Timothy Dudley Smith, based on Psalm 91

Canon Noel Battye and 'Finn' outside St Finnian's Parish Church

15

LIVERPOOL
You'll Never Walk Alone

'O God, our help in ages past,
Our hope for years to come,
Be thou our guard while troubles last,
And our eternal home.'

Isaac Watts

For the last 100 years, Liverpool's seafarers have known they were nearing home when high above them, on a hill overlooking the River Mersey, they could see a great cathedral. It is also a gathering place for the city: in the 1970s, Gerry Marsden sang 'You'll Never Walk Alone' as Liverpool's football fans paid tribute to the legendary Bill Shankly and, in 1982, Pope John Paul II led the people of Liverpool in saying the Lord's prayer.

The 2008 European City of Culture's greatest claim to fame may be as the birthplace of four young boys who once sang pop songs in the Cavern Club in the 1960s, but its Anglican Cathedral is linked to another cathedral by a street called Hope. Together they have become national celebrities, uniting Catholics and Protestants in the fight against poverty and bringing Christian hope both to the city and to the wider world.

The foundation stone for the first cathedral of the Anglican Diocese of Liverpool was laid by King Edward VII on 19 July 1904. It would take seventy-four years to build, so long that a *Punch* cartoon featured an anxious clergyman showing a friend the unfinished building and wondering, 'which will be finished first, the cathedral or organised religion?' In 1964 I stood and watched as an ancient tripod crane lifted stones to form the lowest part of a window in the porch, where Elizabeth Frink's sixteen-foot high bronze sculpture 'the Welcoming Christ' now stands. I did not believe then that the cathedral would ever be finished.

One of many stonemasons and scaffolders who spent their entire working life on the new building was Dame Thora Hird's uncle. Like its architect and many others who worked on it, he did not live to see the completion of the cathedral, but on 25 October 1978, in the presence of the Queen, the cathedral was at last declared complete. Prayers were offered 'for all who have given heart and mind and hand' forever to belong to 'The Company' of the largest Anglican cathedral in Britain, and one of the largest in the world.

The Anglican Cathedral Church of Christ, Liverpool

In 1903, a twenty-two-year-old Roman Catholic, Giles Gilbert Scott, was chosen from a shortlist of five architects to build Liverpool's first cathedral – for the Church of England. It was to be laid out in the shape of a huge double-armed cross, and because of the restricted space at the top of St James's Mount, was to be built in an unconventional north/south alignment.

The lady chapel was completed first, in 1910, big enough to be a large parish church with its own organ and separate entrance. It was the only part of the cathedral influenced by G.F. Bodley, a Victorian Gothic Revival architect, who had been one of the judges for the competition and who kept an eye on the young winner.

The high altar and the chancel were consecrated in 1924. The original designs included two enormous towers, with the architect twice adding to the height of the final single central tower, completed in 1942. It is 331 feet high, made from sandstone and reinforced concrete, and contains a ring of fourteen bells. It has two lifts. The height of the pillars particularly pleased Liverpool's cricketing bishop, David

Sheppard, by being the exact measurement of a cricket pitch.

In spite of using modern materials, the design of the building draws on all the traditional features of Gothic architecture. There is almost a clear view from the back of the nave of the high altar, backed by a huge gilded reredos and a dramatic carving of the Last Supper, except for an unusual but elegant bridge across the front of the nave. The Dulverton Bridge acts as a superb viewpoint and the best place from which to admire the pattern of colours in the marble floor.

Two enormous stained glass windows help fill the cathedral with daylight: one behind the high altar depicts the Te Deum, *whilst over the entrance porch is the* Benedicite *window. This part of the cathedral, completing the third bay of the nave, was the last to be finished.*

I once spent a whole night 'locked up' in Liverpool Cathedral. I had joined hundreds of other young people from churches around the UK invited to the cathedral in the summer of 1973. I was there to do research for a new TV series made by and for young people, which would show their vision of the 'church of the future'. For one night Liverpool Cathedral would be the centre of 'youth culture' – an idea that is commonplace now but which then was as likely as John, Paul, George and Ringo appearing on *Songs of Praise* in the 1960s.

What could this vast, still unfinished, building offer to a new generation impatient to change the world? We were to use the time to argue our corners, to pray together and to be still. There was only one condition: we must stay together until dawn, when the famous campaigner for racial and social justice, Archbishop Trevor Huddleston, would lead worship.

But for all the enthusiasm on offer, by 2.30 a.m. the cathedral just seemed forbidding, dark and cold. Even the most revolutionary and dynamic speakers were losing their audience, and many people had laid out sleeping bags. As I lay down on the hard marble floor of the nave with every muscle beginning to ache, a student in scruffy jeans came over and confided that as he had been denied having his say, he would now wake up the Church of England by playing the cathedral's organ. 'Listen carefully,' he said as he disappeared into the gloom.

I expected a few notes of disgruntled improvisation. But what followed was a complete surprise; he began playing the tune of Isaac Watt's old hymn, 'O God our help in ages past' very quietly, as if it were a lullaby.

'A thousand ages in
thy sight
Are like an evening
gone,
Short as the watch that ends the night
Before the rising sun.'

If a few of us were initially lulled to sleep, all of us must have been wide awake by the time he had finished. 'St Anne' swelled verse by verse, getting louder and louder. Every one of the 9,704 pipes in the largest organ in Britain were being used at one moment or another, and by the triumphant conclusion it felt as if they were together sounding a trumpet call loud enough to wake the living and the dead – and perhaps even the Church of England.

Nobody since has ever been able to tell me who the virtuoso performer was, but Giles Gilbert Scott's cathedral had once again lived up to its reputation for being a space for drama and new thinking. I had shared an experience that would have delighted the first dean of Liverpool, Frederick Dwelly. In his day, a reporter from the Liverpool *Daily Post* wrote, 'The most beautiful cathedral in the world is cold and lifeless unless the Spirit of God acting through the spirits of the living fills it with the warmth and power of love.'

When he arrived in 1930, Canon 'Organizer' Dwelly, or 'Ceremonarius' as he preferred to be known, seemed to know instinctively how to draw people in and use the huge space for worship. He encouraged the congregation to sing, and although he used the traditional *Book of Common Prayer*, he also created many new services. On Easter Day 1937, several thousand people had to be turned away for one such service. Years before *Songs of*

Praise, a choir formed of 1,955 singers and taken from most of Liverpool's churches and chapels came together for an ecumenical service, 'An Affirmation of those who call themselves Christians'. This was an astonishing event for a city where sectarianism was then rife.

Many services have been broadcast by the BBC, but not always to universal approval. One listener wrote angrily, 'We are not to be taken in by all this shrieking and shouting and thumping on the organ – it only gets on our nerves.'

Songs of Praise has come from the cathedral many times, but it is a particular programme in the 1970s, directed by Stuart Cross who was later to become Bishop of Blackburn, that I remember best. In the forty-five year history of *Songs of Praise*, the 1,000 year old legacy of cathedrals created by architects who had never heard of television has often brought the camera-director to their knees, even one destined to be a bishop. Stuart, who loved to experiment, had made a beeline for the enormous cathedral where a successor to Dean Dwelly, Edward Patey, was then using the building as a 'workshop for the Kingdom of God'.

Stuart planned to begin with 'O God, our help in ages past' after a dramatic fanfare from the trumpeters of the Merseyside Police Band, positioned high up on a gallery. They were destined to be heard but not seen, for

Stuart had insisted on a new innovative camera platform so low that only an occasional flash from the spikes of the helmets of the band gave away their location behind the architect's high balustrades.

In 1978, the *Songs of Praise* cameras and the trumpets were present once again, for the dedication service, and this time the shots were perfect. The then Bishop David Sheppard, drawing together all the 'Company', including perhaps the mystery organist, and all the *Songs of Praise* team, dedicated the cathedral with this prayer:

'Blessed be thy name, O Lord, that it hath pleased Thee to put into the hearts of thy servants to erect this house to thine honour and worship. Accept the work of their hands. Remember them concerning this. And grant that all who may enjoy the benefits of this pious work may show forth their thankfulness to Thee by making a right use of the same to the glory of Thy blessed Name.'

16

LIVERPOOL

Paddy's Wigwam

*'**T**he ancient temple was made only for the god; the cathedral is made for all. Vast high, protected by its vaults, amply lit, it shelters all its children who come there to hide, to seek reassurance or information. It houses the magnificent liturgical processions, religious dramas and popular feasts, while the echoing reverberations of the organ, and the Gregorian chants leap upwards and rise to the summit in luminous spirals.'*

Marcel Aubert

Just a five-minute walk from the Anglican Cathedral is Sir Frederick Gibberd's cathedral for Liverpool's Roman Catholic Archdiocese. This short walk was made famous in 1982 when the late Pope John Paul II made his way between the two cathedrals that stand at each end of a street named Hope.

More than fifty years ago, I decided that when I grew up I would be an architect. Every day, walking home from school, my best friend Christopher and I would inspect the emerging shape of a new church. Our Victorian

Victorian parish church had been destroyed in the Second World War, but watching the new church being built to a traditional design, we were sure that we had far better ideas, and dreamed up a grandiose scheme for a cathedral for our suburb. We decided that it would be all concrete and glass, and would create a huge space for processions in order to transform the dull lives of our neighbours. And if only the builders would use these new ideas, it could all be done so much more quickly and cheaply, we thought.

Little did we know that on a hill above the River Mersey, far from the daily site-meetings of two schoolboys who were bottom equal of their class in mathematics and hardly knew what the word 'economics' meant, such ideas were already taking shape for a second cathedral for Liverpool.

The Metropolitan Cathedral of Christic the King, Liverpool

In 1930, Liverpool's Roman Catholics bought some land on Brownlow Hill, above the city centre and less than a mile from the growing bulk of the Anglican Cathedral. It had originally been the site of Liverpool's workhouse, where at one time over half the destitute who found shelter there had been Irish Catholic immigrants. In fact, caring for the needs of Liverpool's poor was one reason why for eighty years after the restoration of Catholic bishops in England, the city still did not have a cathedral. The architect Sir Edwin Lutyens, best known for the Cenotaph, the nation's memorial to the war dead, drew up plans for an enormous basilica topped by a dome that would rise nearly 200 feet above the tower of the Anglican Cathedral. The foundation stone was laid on Whit

Monday, 1933, but by 1941 only the huge crypt was finished. War and rising costs had brought work to a halt.

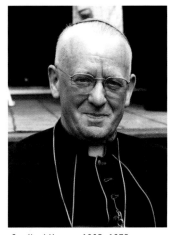

Cardinal Heenan 1905–1975

It had been the dream of one of Liverpool's first archbishops, Cardinal Heenan, that the building would be a 'cathedral for our time'. In 1959, 300 architects from both Britain and around the world were invited to come up with entirely new designs to fit the spirit of the age, just as the Catholic Church was itself beginning a revolution in its liturgy. It was quite a challenge: not only must the building cost no more than a million pounds, a fraction of Lutyen's original estimate, but it had to be built on top of his crypt. The man who won the competition was Frederick Gibberd, and from October 1962, his extraordinary concrete building, which looked like an enormous wigwam, began to rise into the sky.

Using revolutionary construction techniques, Gibberd created a vast circular space to enclose the altar – the heart of his cathedral. Gathered around it for mass, worshippers would no longer witness a remote event. The altar, a single block of marble weighing twenty tons and dug out of the ground in what was then Yugoslavia, was to be placed under a lantern tower. Daylight filtering through its vivid stained glass would fall as the light of heaven on to the altar and its fragile bronze figure of Christ designed by the sculptor, Elisabeth Frink, showing his arms outstretched as much in compassion and welcome as in the agony of the Cross.

On 14 May 1967, a century after the first designs were drawn up, the English city with the largest Catholic population finally had a cathedral to call its own. As the late Cardinal Heenan wrote, 'It is my belief that the prayers of the people of Liverpool were more responsible for the winning design than the assessors or, for all we know, than the architect himself.' In 1959, the letter inviting architects to submit their designs had ended with the line, 'the priests and people of the archdiocese of Liverpool will beg God to enlighten you.' On that day in 1967, on the Feast of Pentecost, they had their answer.

The service of consecration and the solemn processions from the streets into the huge concrete tent were shown on the BBC. The watching Liverpudlians christened it 'Paddy's Wigwam'.

It does not take long to experience the ecumenical spirit that links Liverpool's two cathedrals, the natural relationship that led to Pope John Paul II's visit to both buildings in 1982. When I walk down Hope Street to meet Sister Anthony MBE in Paddy's Wigwam, I come carrying affectionate greetings from Geoff Shipley, one of the guides in the Anglican Cathedral.

To find Sister Anthony, the driving force behind a team of sixty volunteers ranging in age from eleven to eighty-six, whose needlecraft has created many beautiful banners and decorations for churches, I have been led down into the Lutyens crypt. I hear her team long before I see them, for Sister Anthony's team of stitchers seem frequently to be in stitches as they work away in the most relaxed atmosphere that I have ever experienced within a cathedral crypt.

The atmosphere has not always been so calm for Sister Anthony. Not long after she retired from teaching and took on the job of artistic director within the cathedral, her baptism of fire came: the visit of Pope John Paul II. Thirty-six sets of red vestments were needed for various cardinals and bishops, and it was her team that had to make them. Finishing just in time, she was suddenly given the most unnerving job when, at the very last minute, her boss appeared with the Pope's own silk vestments which, having travelled with him, were in urgent need of an iron. She worked as fast as she could

Sister Anthony with the late Pope John Paul II's vestments

on her little ironing board within the crypt, whilst the congregation waited for the great moment when the Pope would appear in his finery. The fragile garment duly ironed, it was given afterwards to the cathedral where it now takes pride of place in her workroom.

Sister Anthony brims with energy and enthusiasm as she circles the tables where more than two dozen people are hard at work with needle and thread. But she can't resist breaking off to see if her visitor is happy. In spite of my messy appearance, towing a suitcase and with armfuls of carrier bags, I am treated as an honoured guest. This remarkable nun, who tells me that she is eighty-two, is a great fan of *Songs of Praise* and always telephones her friend Pam Rhodes immediately after her every appearance.

She talks about her favourite saint, Teresa of Avila. 'Descend with your mind into your heart, and stand in the presence of the Lord.' This seems to be the secret of Sister Anthony's own art, as she pencil-sketches her first tiny designs for a new set of huge banners to be hung in the cathedral. With the title Epiphany and Star, she wants to show the three kings in a boat, leaving safe harbour to head into a storm.

When Sister Anthony sends me on my way, she insists that for my own well-being, I am to go up into the cathedral taking the sloping ramp which Gibberd designed so that at the beginning of every mass, both choir and clergy could literally rise up out of the crypt. I must have been, however, the first person to appear up the cathedral's wonderful processional way pulling a battered suitcase with squeaky wheels.

But the experience is worth my self-conscious embarrassment. The artist in the crypt knows that as I creep up the slope into Paddy's Wigwam, all the colours of the rainbow from the afternoon light

flooding through the stained glass and falling on my head will act as my own epiphany.

'Fear not to enter his courts in the slenderness
Of the poor wealth thou would'st reckon as
   thine:
Truth in its beauty, and love in its tenderness,
These are the offerings to lay on his shrine.'

J.S.B. Monsell 1811–1875

Looking down Hope Street towards 'Paddy's Wigwam' in 1967

17

MANCHESTER
Church Without Walls

*'I have just taken part in the first **Daily Service of the British Broadcasting Company**. It occupied less than a quarter of an hour but during that brief space of time I was in touch with many to whom this newest idea of the BBC will bring real happiness and spiritual comfort every day in the year. Outside, this is a wet and cheerless Monday morning, making the contrast of a lighted room and a seat by a blazing log fire all the stronger.'*

Blackburn Times, *7 January 1928*

On the first weekday of 1928, Monday 2 January, the BBC broadcast a live service from the studio in London's Savoy Hill. Listeners heard the Revd H.L. Johnston introducing a hymn, a psalm, a Bible reading and some prayers. This broadcast marked the conclusion of a long campaign by a listener to persuade the BBC to include a religious service in their output every single day.

This was an extraordinary demonstration of audience power. The idea of viewers requesting hymns from *Songs of Praise* for Dame Thora Hird's *Praise Be*, or voting in a poll for The Nation's Favourite Hymn, would never have been countenanced by the austere Scots Presbyterian, John Reith, the man who helped to create the Corporation. The BBC's first director-general was not in the habit of being told by his listeners what should be broadcast; the BBC did not even at the time possess an audience research department.

Miss Kathleen Cordeux, listening at home in Watford, broke through the director-general's defences with a steady flow of letters, backed by a petition signed by 5,000 people. Like them, she had either heard or been with others, possibly the sick, as they listened to the broadcasts of choral evensong that the BBC was transmitting once a week. She wrote, 'Only those who watch the expression on the face of sufferers when they are listening to a message from Above through the wireless can imagine what it would mean to them.'

The Daily Service is still broadcast on Radio 4 more than seventy-five years later, and on at least one occasion has been seen on television, although the producers say that nothing can beat the power of radio to create the best 'pictures'. And for a congregation now numbered in hundreds of thousands, who join in services from their living room, their car, their hospital bed or even their bath, the nation's favourite church is in a leafy suburb of south Manchester: Emmanuel Church, Didsbury.

The Parish Church of St James and Emmanuel, Didsbury, Manchester

The Daily Service has had many homes. When Broadcasting House in London opened in 1932, a special studio was provided. Studio 3E was even consecrated, and the presenter sat in a suitably ecclesiastical setting, facing a cross. The studio was destroyed by a wartime bomb, but by then the presenters and singers had been evacuated, first to Bristol

Cathedral and then to St Paul's Church in Bedford. After the war and back in London, the broadcasts moved to All Soul's, Langham Place in 1951. Here for over forty years, the presenters and BBC singers led the nation in worship, battling against the raucous din of one of the capital's busiest streets.

In 1993 the backdrop for the broadcasts moved once again, this time to Manchester and to the quiet surroundings of the only suburban church so far to have become one of the nation's favourites. Here in Didsbury, they were welcomed by a congregation of 400 that had already adapted the late-Victorian church to suit many different styles of worship.

Built out of stone in the popular Gothic Revival style, the church was consecrated on 7 July 1858. The church's treasures include stained glass by the famous artist, Edward Burne Jones, and the golden hue surrounding the figure of 'The Sower' now lights up the Daily Service choir even on a gloomy day. On the vestry walls, forefathers of Victorian respectability such as the Revd Osbert Fynes-Clinton, vicar from 1878–1900, gaze in sepia splendour down upon the high-tech broadcasting equipment.

Emmanuel Church stands round the corner from a row of shops used by people of many cultures who now live in the area. Conventional furnishings in the church have been replaced by modern seats grouped around a rostrum, with a plain table serving as an altar. Four floor panels in the floor cover a pool for full-immersion baptism. A new hall extends this family church further, which also welcomes students from Manchester's two universities.

I am not sure that Miss Cordeux

would approve of listening to the *Daily Service* in the car, and would probably be horrified to learn that I often hear it in the bath. When the broadcasts began, it was the custom in some houses for the servants to be allowed to down tools and assemble respectfully with 'the lady of the house' in front of the wireless. Vicars were supposedly afraid that radio worship might be heard by 'men in pubs wearing their hats' although I think that this is an apocryphal story, unkindly aimed at bewildered clergy who could not cope with the rapidly changing ways of the world. But it is true certainly that Mrs Davidson, wife of the then Archbishop of Canterbury, believed that to hear the radio, the windows of Lambeth Palace needed to be open first. And yet while broadcasting has transformed the way that we understand the world, people today in their eighties have been alive for its entire history.

The Daily Service *starts here*

Christians leading the *Daily Service* today, coping with the technology of the third millennium AD, have to time their worship down to a split second so that they lead the final choir 'Amen' just before the pips of the Greenwich Time Signal herald the ten o'clock news on Radio 4. Woe betide anyone who overruns, and I often find myself offering a hurried prayer when I sense that one of my former colleagues is in danger.

Such a daunting duty requires a disciplined countdown from early morning. Arriving an hour before the broadcast, I find rehearsals well underway. Christopher Stokes, the choirmaster of Manchester Cathedral, is gently but rigorously coaching five women and four men from a team of around two dozen regulars of the *Daily Service* singers. 'I shan't permit any flexibility before the Amen,' he warns.

The singers, who are all volunteers from the area and selected both for vocal ability and Christian commitment, are gathered around today's presenter, who sits at a small table. Becky Harris is from one of the youngest generations to lead broadcasts that former controller of Radio 4, James Boyle, describes as 'part of the deepest traditions of Britain, on a par with christening a child or crowning a monarch'.

Becky wears earphones which allow her to take instructions from the producer, Mark O'Brien, based with the control equipment in a sort of small cupboard off the vestry with the technicians, Steve and Michael. A reassuring presence, Mark pads around suggesting script changes and even leaves his cupboard in the middle of the live broadcast to read the story of Mary and Martha from St John's Gospel.

Even though there can be no room for mistakes, the atmosphere is very laid-back.

At one point, the rehearsal stops and the choir vanish for coffee. Nerve-wrackingly for me, they do not reappear until it is close to the time that the broadcast must begin. Meanwhile I sit alone with four microphones and a row of empty chairs, wondering what I should do if *Start the Week* ends early. It is all so unlike television where for up to half-an-hour before a live broadcast of *Songs of Praise*, a tense countdown worthy of the launch of a space shuttle proceeds, and producer, presenter and performers shed many pounds in weight.

But suddenly, everyone is back in place, looking intently at the conductor for the signal to begin. Becky has donned her headphones and another *Daily Service* goes out live on the air. Ironically, Becky has chosen to begin with Rudyard Kipling's poem 'If' – 'If you can keep your head when all about you are losing theirs…'

'*Lord, you have given much to your children, but give us one thing more: a thankful heart. Not just thankful when it pleases, as though your mercies had spare days, but a thankful heart whose very pulse may be to live to your praise. Amen.*'

A prayer of George Herbert adapted by the late Ron Farrow, former presenter of the Daily Service

18

SHREWSBURY
Travellers' Tales

'There, if I mistake not, is the valley through which our future friend the railway runs. Yes! And there you may catch the shining rails themselves running along their gravelly bed.

How lamentably unromantic is every thing and every one becoming! We must throw in our lot with others, and submit to be whirled on with the rest of the world.'

From A Church Tour through England and Wales *by John Mason Neale*

Terry Barlow, a listener to BBC Radio Shropshire, nominated 'a little Pugin gem' as one of the nation's favourites, the Roman Catholic cathedral within his hometown of Shrewsbury.

The direct route south from Cheshire to Shrewsbury seems to take the traveller back in time. This is a Britain of fifty years ago, before motorways, a Britain of black and white photography taken from the *Country Life Picture Book of Britain* that once had the power to transport me from winter gloom to summer dreams. Ancient hedgerows line a road that twists and turns, and only by steering towards a watery sun do I feel hopeful that I am heading for Shrewsbury.

But this is not only the lost land of mail coaches and olde inns where horses might still be changed overnight. By pure chance, the road south to Shrewsbury takes me past one of England's long lost railway destinations, Coole Pilate. These outposts on the system that were regarded with such suspicion by John Mason Neale held almost as much fascination for John Betjeman as did the wayside parish church. In 1963 Dr Beeching, the arch-betrayer of the branch railway line, swept the Halt with its most biblical of names into oblivion. I had always wondered where it was, and why it was not in the litany of exotic names included in the wistful song 'Slow Train'

written by Flanders and Swann, a farewell to the country's railway. But also, why does the church not appear in any guide?

There is a sign welcoming me to Coole Pilate. But not only is there no trace of a railway station, there is not even a trace of a village. For the next thirty minutes, I keep finding myself returning to this road sign. The only clue is a mysterious notice directing me to the 'Secret Bunker', presumably a high-security establishment less in need of seclusion than the village itself. The obvious solution is to find the church – surely a gnarled old building smelling of ancient hymnbooks and hassocks is waiting for the passing pilgrim somewhere in this green and pleasant land? The answer, however, seems to be 'no'. According to the records, Coole Pilate is not a parish but 'a township'. One also without a church, and so, having driven round in circles, I now arrive late at Shrewsbury's Roman Catholic Cathedral.

The Cathedral Church of Our Lady, Help of Christians and of St Peter of Alcantara, Shrewsbury

The Roman Catholic Diocese of Shrewsbury was created in September 1850, and six years later on 28 October, the cathedral was consecrated. Built on the town walls, near where friars and monks had lived in Pre-Reformation times, it was a more modest building than originally planned through the unexpected expense of having to dig seventy feet down in order to find firm ground. As a result, the little cathedral is scarcely as tall as it is deep. The architect, Edward Welby Pugin, was only eighteen when he was appointed, taking over from his famous father, Augustus Pugin, who had been admitted to a

mental hospital before dying a year later. The cathedral is built in the then fashionable Gothic Revival style, trademark of the work of the Pugin family.

Inside, the eye is drawn to the huge hanging rood of 1885. This replaced a simpler cross carved from an old pear tree that was growing on the site of the new building. The pear tree has its own memorial, for in the stained glass of the east window, Our Lady holds a pear. Under the rood is the altar, carved in 1985 from a single block of local stone. Behind the altar is the bishop's seat, the 'cathedra', which by tradition is the seat on which he sits to teach his diocese, hence the name cathedral.

The modern organ is in the west gallery, the base for a very active choir and music group to which Terry Barlow, who nominated the cathedral, belongs.

Much of the stained glass was designed by the artist Margaret Rope, a local woman who became a Carmelite nun. Amongst the six windows depicting the martyrs of England, including Thomas à Becket and Thomas More, is one commemorating a great meeting of English Catholics in London in 1921, and even includes a London bus!

'Being held up by a builder's skip arriving, and moving cars around our tiny car park is not the best preparation for mass – but it's my only excuse for us starting late,' says Fr Paul, as he begins the weekday lunchtime service. 'But you have come here too with your own troubles and joys, so welcome!'

It places Fr Paul into the ranks of those priests and ministers who retain the uncanny knack of knowing just how his congregation feel about the day so far. I have also spent much of my visit meditating on the problems of parking in the beautiful narrow streets around the cathedral, and as we waited for Fr Paul to appear, I had begun to imagine traffic wardens prowling around my car as time began to run out on the meter.

Looking around the small congregation, I can see that I am not the only traveller present. Two young women

have parked huge suitcases by their seats, and a student with the ubiquitous backpack with which it seems people now travel the world has finally sat down, having previously scrutinized every nook and cranny of the building; a Filipino boy, meanwhile, kneels motionless at the statue of Our Lady.

As an Anglican, I find that there is something profoundly compelling about the way that services are always the same in every Roman Catholic church, regardless of where one is in the world. Even in countries where I may not speak the language, the rhythm of the liturgy is familiar and I feel at home. Entries in the Shrewsbury visitors' book confirm my feeling that a whole world on the move, 'whirled on' as gloomily prophesied by John Mason Neale, still comes to look for rest in churches like this.

This experience was reinforced by two months spent in New Zealand, after my visit here to Shrewsbury. Living next door to a Roman Catholic chapel, a steady stream of international callers would call in and ask when the services were held. The visitors' book there recorded many travellers listed, from Britain to the Shrine of St Peter Chanel on the faraway shores of the South Pacific. For 'Gillian and Barry from Norfolk', one couple listed for example, the little chapel in New Zealand became 'an oasis' on their journey.

While I was in the cathedral in Shrewsbury, a woman originally from Germany stopped to talk to me. It seemed that her travelling days were done forty years ago because she had been at mass in this cathedral every day since. This was her home now, and here, she said, 'my tree has spread'.

'Longing for light, we wait in darkness
Longing for truth, we turn to you.
Make us your own, your holy people
Light for the world to see.
Christ be our light!
Shine in our hearts
Shine through the darkness
Christ be our light!
Shine in your church
Gathered today.'

Bernadette Farrell

19

NEW SELSTON
The Little Chapel Near the Railway

*'**S**ee how great a flame aspires,*
Kindled by a spark of grace!
Jesu's love the nations fires,
Sets the kingdoms on a blaze.
To bring fire on earth He came;
Kindled in some hearts it is:
O that all might catch the flame,
All partake the glorious bliss!'

Charles Wesley

New Selston Chapel is not listed in one of those 'just off the motorway' guides that one has while breaking a long journey. But it should be, especially for Sunday travellers on the M1 who are passing through Nottinghamshire. Here is a true survivor, one of a fast dwindling number of small and simple non-conformist chapels, where generations of families have found faith on their doorstep.

'Hello, luv! Would you like to see inside our chapel?' A small figure was at my side on the pavement, arriving so silently that I almost jumped out of my skin. So began a visit to a beautifully cared for primitive Methodist chapel, built in 1904. Led by my guide, Mrs Evelyn Marshall who as well as caretaker is the treasurer, pianist (some times) and 'giver-out of hymnbooks' (most times), I was made to feel as if I was in her home. Equally, it could have

been the New Jerusalem, as she showed me the building that she loves and where she first came aged three (and that, as she told me, was eighty-five years ago).

To tell the truth, I had turned off the motorway on my way south to Leicestershire only because, as a diehard lifelong railway enthusiast, I had caught a glimpse of an old signal box with semaphore signals and sidings. Such things are of a bygone age that never see or are seen by the new generation of high-speed trains. At the bottom of the valley and at the end of the village of Pinxton, it appeared, a fine Midland Railway signal box and as ornately decorated as any church of the Edwardian era. But as the car bounced across the rusting rails at the level crossing, I was unknowingly entering another country – New Selston.

Methodist Chapel, New Selston

In this Nottinghamshire mining village, not long after the death of Queen Victoria in 1901, an open-air meeting was held in a field, conducted by a young man named Mr C. Hogg. Pledged to the Christian life, he had recently arrived to work at the Langton Colliery. At this service when, it is recorded, 'much to the surprise of everyone, all the mothers and fathers with the children were present', the young man said that he wanted to establish a Methodist church at New Selston.

There were other Methodist chapels in the district, one just across the railway line, but Mr Hogg was a 'Primitive' Methodist, a division of Methodism that infuriated the mainstream church by preferring to worship in the open air rather than join existing chapels or become part of the hierarchical structures of Wesleyan Methodism. Primitive Methodism was not to be united with the Wesleyan 'connection' until 1932. Indeed this movement, begun in nearby Staffordshire by William Clowes and Hugh Bourne, the latter a carpenter with 'a zeal for open air meetings', was not recognized at all before 1811, when their first chapel was built. Their so-called 'camp meetings' in the open air were described by a leading Wesleyan as 'highly improper and likely to be of considerable mischief.'

However, young Mr Hogg from the colliery at Selston was evidently a persuasive Christian because he had soon

persuaded the owner of the field to allow her stables to be used for worship and, with the gift of a stove and a small organ, 'the first of many grand services was held'. Sleepers were somehow 'acquired' from the railway to be used as a floor for a new hut. Another lady must also have been persuaded by Mr Hogg to dramatically repent and change her ways, for at a time when all Methodism was synonymous with temperance and when to travel by rail on the sabbath was severely frowned upon ('a most wilful and reckless abuse of providence by sabbath-breakers and reprobates' fumed a writer in The Cottager's Monthly Visitor), it was the landlady of the Railway Inn, a Miss Cooper, who provided a pulpit and attended the first Sunday service.

The present chapel was completed in October 1904. The miners of the village coming off many long shifts in the pit dug the foundations, individuals donated bricks (their names are still visible in the wall by the entrance) and when finished, the women came with buckets and scrubbing brushes to clean the new building. And in the fine tradition of Methodism, after the opening service there was a huge tea party thrown for the whole village, to celebrate the results of real sacrifice by a community of working people that had no rich benefactors to call upon.

The simple interior remains very much as it was built, as spic and span as it was on the opening day just over a century ago. 'A small Bethel in a little corner of the village, but its worship is warm and its zeal is strong,' said the anonymous writer of a booklet celebrating the sixtieth anniversary. The colliery today is long closed, together with most traditional manufacturing in the area, but whereas so many little chapels are today video rental stores, carpet warehouses or even weekend cottages, New Selston Chapel survives.

'As long as I have the strength and the key to the door, the chapel will be open,' said Mrs Marshall as she led me in. I said what I felt, 'what a quiet, restful and beautiful space.' 'Do you think so?' asked my host with a piercing gaze that would unmask any insincerity. It is indeed beautiful in a simple and direct way. Full of light and immediately homely, the mystery of the grace of God, which John Wesley felt on the night when his heart was 'strangely warmed', still pervades the place.

Mrs Marshall showed me the pew where she sat for the very first time when brought to a service. She still sits in the same pew, but at the other end now, perhaps because of a moment that she will never forget.

'Who wants to be a missionary? asked the minister at the time. Up went the three-year-old Evelyn's hand.

'Very good, I'll be round tomorrow to see your mother and we'll make the arrangements!' said the minister. Mrs Marshall remembers that she hid in terror for quite a while afterwards, every time someone knocked on the door.

I sensed that this stalwart of her church had been through as many ups and downs as the building itself. 'Often there are as few as ten of us for the service,' she says, 'and I sit and look at where the others used to be.' Mrs Marshall even left the congregation herself for a time, although she didn't tell me why. 'I just went out and slammed the door but I couldn't find peace.' So she returned. When her husband died, she took over from him as treasurer.

Any idea I might have had that I was in some distant outpost of Methodism was quickly dispelled when Mrs Marshall revealed that she was quite up to date with the workings of the Methodist Conference and had been at the debates about the new covenant with the Church of England in 2004. She was also looking forward to the arrival of a new woman minister in the Methodist Circuit who would be coming to New Selston.

I felt cheered up by my visit to New Selston. Although she had never travelled to another country as a missionary, in the end Mrs Marshall had become a missionary of sorts, to me at least.

Mission Praise is the hymnbook now used at New Selston, but when young Evelyn volunteered to be the youngest-ever missionary, they might well have been singing the old mission hymn, 'See how great a flame aspires'. Written by Charles Wesley, it is number 491 in the *Methodist School Hymnal* and sung to the tune, 'St

Mrs Evelyn Marshall in the pew where she first sat when she was three years old

George's Windsor' (now usually set to the words of 'Come ye thankful people, come' at harvest time). It has all the classic Wesley imagery, who himself began his ministry preaching to crowds in the open air.

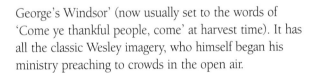

'Saw ye not the cloud arise,
Little as a human hand?
Now it spreads along the skies,
Hangs o'er all the thirsty land:
Lo! The promise of a shower
Drops already from above;
But the Lord will shortly pour
All the Spirit of his Love!'

Charles Wesley

ENDERBY

Our Vicar is a Pirate!

*'**T**he Country Parson preacheth constantly, the pulpit is his joy and his throne… When he preacheth, he procures attention by all possible art, both by earnestness of speech, it being natural to men to think, that where there is much earnestness, there is somewhat worth hearing; and by a diligent, and busy cast of his eye on his auditors, with letting them know, that he observes who marks, and who not; and with particularizing of his speech now to the younger sort, then to the elder. This is for you, and this is for you; for particulars ever touch and awake more generals… for people are very attentive at such discourses, and think it behoves them to do so, when God is so neer them, and even over their heads.'*

from A Priest to the Temple or the Country Parson
by George Herbert 1611

When young Jim Hawkins, hero of Robert Louis Stevenson's *Treasure Island*, first encounters wild Ben Gunn, a castaway on a desert island, he is told that solitude has had its reward. 'It were Providence that put me here. I've thought it all out in this 'ere lonely island, and I'm back on piety.'

Gunn has even made his own church at the spot where his six comrades, murdered by wicked Captain Flint, lie buried. 'I've come here and prayed, now and then, when I thought maybe a Sunday would be about due. It weren't quite a chapel, but it seemed more solemn like; and then Ben Gunn was short-handed – no chaplain, nor so much as a Bible and a flag.'

'Turn left at the traffic lights and look out for the pirates!' These are my only directions for finding the Revd Steve Davies, clerk in holy orders and vicar of St John the Baptist Parish Church, Enderby, nominated as one of the nation's favourite churches by a listener to BBC Radio Leicester.

From the outside, it looks like thousands of other Victorian churches, although its car park seems surprisingly full for a Friday afternoon. Inside, children are rushing around noisily as a gang of strong men build a scene across the chancel, turning it into a theatre set for Stevenson's *Treasure Island*. In the middle of the melee a man stands in a three-cornered hat and a black frock coat with lacy sleeves, Captain Steve Davies of the pirate ship *Hispaniola*. In charge of creating order out of chaos, he hopes also to bring about the transformation of an old church at the centre of a middle England village.

'I am young enough to be impatient,' he says, standing back to survey the afternoon's work, which has successfully concealed all the traditional features of Victorian church furnishings. He pulls off his ridiculous hat, becoming more reflective. 'But I also want the church to be like an apple tree growing slowly and quietly and I want to serve this church for the rest of my days.'

Many old church guidebooks bear witness to this kind of ministry, although long-serving clergy in the eighteenth century were often absent from the parish, sometimes living comfortably abroad for years on end as Anthony Trollope so aptly described in the *Barchester* novels. A lot of parish churches have gilded boards up that record just how many of their beloved vicars remained in position for decades. But until I met Steve, however, I wouldn't have believed that any young clergyman would have this kind of game plan today. But by the end of my visit, I came to understand a little better why he feels called to be a long term part of what, with great affection, he calls 'little old Enderby'.

The Parish Church of
St John the Baptist, Enderby

All that is left of the medieval parish church of Enderby is the tower built in the thirteenth century. A local benefactor in what was then a busy stone-quarrying village funded a complete rebuilding in 1867, and the parishioners provided a magnificent Victorian font. A stained glass window of St George commemorates Victoria's Golden Jubilee of 1887. There is even a very rare survivor of something invented during her reign, installed before the days of electricity and intended to help the hard-of-hearing members of the congregation. In the

desk of the vicar's stall in the chancel is a sliding panel, and inside is a horn, connected by piping to a set of ear-trumpets in a pew in the south aisle. These 'whispering tubes for extreme deafness' are relics of the Victorian thirst for innovation. F. Charles Rein and Son's 'New Acoustic Instrument' was apparently adapted from a patent system of 'Conversation Tubes for Railway Conveyances'.

Until 2003, the church would have been completely familiar to worshippers at the time of Queen Victoria. But in 2003 a new innovation, planned for over a decade, saw most of the pews replaced by new, comfortable chairs and the whole church carpeted. Four meeting rooms, a kitchen area and loos were created out of the north aisle and the tower.

'For many people, church can seem rather daunting and

'Where your treasure is there your heart will be also.' Steve has borrowed this from Matthew, using it as a headline for his summer 'Holiday Bible Club'.

'Along with the other churches in Enderby, we will be pirates searching for treasure.' So even though we are almost as far from the sea as anyone can be in England, Stevenson's famous mystery and adventure about pirates is being used to help the children of the village glimpse the Bible through new eyes. Meanwhile, the church computer links 'little old Enderby' with Moore College in Australia, as Steve's older parishioners study online and journey in faith with those who have found treasure in the Bible as well as a new life on the other side of the world.

I had always thought that the inspiration for *Treasure Island* was an island off the coast of East Lothian in Scotland, where Stevenson wrote many of his novels, until last year. It was then that I saw for myself the many little islands of the Pacific and read about some of the nineteenth-century Christian missionaries that Stevenson, who himself died in Samoa in the South Pacific, would certainly have known about. Indeed, he would have had to brave seas policed partly by pirates in order to reach Samoa.

On Christmas Day 1814, Samuel Marsden from Yorkshire became the first missionary to conduct Christian worship in the Bay of Islands. On New Zealand's North Island, the service had a mixed congregation of Europeans and 'their dark fellow-creatures'. For both the incomers and the Maori, whose lands they had often purchased in exchange for guns, these were turbulent days with many dashed hopes and betrayals on both sides.

When Marsden sailed back into the Bay twenty-five years later, he wrote, 'The contrast between the east and west side of the bay was very striking; the east shore was crowded with different tribes of fighting men, in a wild savage state, many of them nearly naked. Nothing was to

Samuel Marsden, 1765–1835

be heard but the firing of muskets, and the din and confusion of a savage military camp; some mourning the death of their friends, others suffering from their wounds; and not one whose mind was not involved in heathen darkness, without one ray of divine knowledge.

'On the west side, there was the pleasing sound of the "church-going bell"; the natives assembling together for Divine Worship, clean, orderly, and decently dressed: they were carrying in their hands the greater part of the Church Service with the hymns, written in their own language. Here might be viewed, at one glance, the blessings of the Christian Religion, and the miseries of Heathenism, with respect to the present life: but when we direct our thoughts into the Eternal World, how infinite is the difference!'

Steve Davies sees himself as a modern missionary, and though his twenty-first century mission draws no distinction between age, creed or race, he speaks with the same urgency. 'Six thousand people live in Enderby and the most that are ever in our four churches are 300.' He pauses and looks around. 'So ninety-five per cent of the [local] population are facing a Christless eternity. A danger of being in hell? Now that's serious.'

Since visiting Enderby, I have read for the first time the words of Fanny Crosby's famous mission hymn, 'Rescue the perishing'. This hymn has almost certainly never been sung on *Songs of Praise*, but it formed the punchline of a story told often by one of the programme's first researchers, Revd Frank Pagden. While at BBC Radio Leeds, he organized a radio version of *Dial a Hymn*, a programme that I later produced for ITV. Frank always claimed that he had a Salvation Army band ready in the street outside the studio, so that when a listener phoned in for this particular hymn, he called out of the window: 'Right lads, "Rescue the perishing" – and be quick about it!'

Having met the Vicar of Enderby, I think I have finally got the point.

'Rescue the perishing,
Duty demands it:
Strength for thy labour the Lord will
    provide:
Back to the narrow way
Patiently win them;
Tell the poor wanderer a Saviour has
    died.
Rescue the perishing,
Care for the dying;
Jesus is merciful, Jesus will save.'

Fanny Crosby

Steve Davies, vicar and 'pirate' of Enderby

DOWN HATHERLEY
Only the Wanderer Knows England's Graces

'The church visitor, with his knapsack on his back, his sketch-book, and note-book, and foot-rule, and measuring-tape in his pocket, his good oak stick in his hand, with fair weather, and a fine tract of churches before him, is the happiest – and so, the freest of human beings.'

A Church Tour through England and Wales *in 1843*
by John Mason Neale

Chris Brind likes the 'localness' of BBC Radio Gloucester's religious programmes, and nominated the local church that he knows best. In the village of Down Hatherley, where he 'married a spinster of this parish', he is a churchwarden of the church of St Mary and Corpus Christi.

But passing through the lychgate into a well-tended graveyard, I find myself in a mid-Victorian time warp. This little church, in the middle of the Gloucestershire countryside, feels as if John Mason Neale himself might have been here until a few minutes ago.

Well, almost. It was not a nineteenth-century visitor that demolished the church fence. 'Did you do that?' asks a man standing by the church door, who has observed my clumsy parking. He turns out not to be churchwarden Chris Brind whom I am coming to meet but instead a kindly builder who has come to inspect a leak in the church roof. Getting into the church, literally 'by the back door' courtesy of another man, who also turns out not to be Chris, is to witness the unlocking of a church that rivals Fort Knox for its security. In spite of all the keys and bolts, however, and although I have never met either of them before, I am welcomed in. I am left wondering if there are any places other than churches where the total stranger is so trusted.

We enter the church from behind the organ, some of whose pipes seem to go right through the roof. Water is coming in at the most vulnerable spot and there is an obvious risk to the clearly cherished instrument built in 1924 by Jackson of Oxford, one of the features that make Down Hatherley Parish Church such a popular choice for weddings. I finally track down the nominee, Chris Brind, tending graves in the churchyard with his wife. As he soon tells me, the small church inside has a warm and intimate feel to it.

The Parish Church of St Mary and Corpus Christi, Down Hatherley

The church was constructed in the fifteenth century, but now the medieval late-perpendicular tower at the west end is all that remains of the original structure. In 1859, work began on a complete rebuild supervised by F. S. Waller. It has been described as one of the architect's best Gothic Revival country

churches. The work was paid for by the family of Sir Matthew Wood, one time Lord Mayor of London.

Brightly coloured stained glass windows by O'Connor were installed in the chancel. Fine encaustic floor tiles were laid, and the late sixteenth-century lead font was set in place on a new stone base. Later stained glass windows in the north aisle record members of the parish who died in the First World War.

Recently a member of the parish, Peter Smith, an engineer by profession, designed and made a new side altar out of American red oak. Produced entirely by traditional methods, this beautiful object brings Down Hatherley Church full circle, with a return to the skills of the medieval craftsman who built the original church.

Outside, in the adjacent glebe field, an abandoned well that once served the church's rectory has been restored in memory of a recent rector, the Revd John O'Brien, who died in office in 2003, having served the parish for eighteen years. But compared with one of his Victorian predecessors, Henry William Maddy, his ministry was over in a flash.

'Leave the church as Canon Maddy had it!' This message from an anonymous source in Down Hatherley is a warning that I know only too well. As a former churchwarden in Kent, the need once to remove woodwormed Victorian pews produced the unsigned but heartfelt scrawl in our visitor's book, 'Do not touch our church!'

The idea of leaving a building in exactly the condition it was in the time of a rector that died in 1907 at first seems absurd. There can be surely no one left alive who

knew Canon Maddy. But you quickly discover that Canon Maddy is still a force to be reckoned with here. From Sir William Bakyn in 1532, through to Samuel Gwinnett, whose oddly-named son Button was a signatory to the American Declaration of Independence in 1776, none have served this parish for as long as Henry William Maddy. He arrived in 1856 as vicar and stayed for fifty-one years, dying in 1907, having outlived Queen Victoria.

Back in 1856, England was in the throes of a different kind of revolution, an economic and industrial one. Four years earlier, the opening of the Great Exhibition in London had been described by *The Times* as 'the first morning since the creation of the world that all peoples have assembled from all parts of the world and done a common act'. The newly-built railway system had ensured that almost nowhere was too remote to visit. But the division between rich and poor was growing, especially in Gloucestershire; wool manufacturing had migrated north and imports from all over the world were threatening local jobs. One contemporary of Canon Maddy, in rural Devonshire, even devoted his ministry to trying to persuade his own parishioners to migrate.

In 1860, Down Hatherley Parish Church had a facelift. This was a scene being repeated in countless other parishes across the country, where a good relationship between a rector and a local benefactor led to dilapidated buildings receiving a Gothic-Revival makeover using all the benefits of modern technology. In Down Hatherley's case, for probably the first time since nearby battles between Cavaliers and Roundheads in 1643, the building was made dry and warm

inside, and lit by stained glass that would have been impossible to afford before the Industrial Revolution. The church was enjoying all the benefits of Victorian progress and invention. If at first an organ was not available, or indeed an organist, it no longer mattered as *'Debain's Antiphonel* – a substitute for an organist, by which a person without the knowledge of music can play the common hymn tunes' – could be purchased for twelve guineas.

Out went higgledy-piggledy box-pews jealously guarded by the local gentry, and in came pews for the poor who traditionally could not pay for seats. But also went the medieval south door through which by tradition, children were brought for baptism. It seems that few medieval churches escaped entirely 'careful restoration' with the Victorian 'machine' taking over the work of the artist. Stone tracery, which had once taken armies of craftsmen weeks to produce, could now be manufactured in great quantity through a steam-powered saw.

It is easy when visiting Down Hatherley to picture the world of the Victorian country parson and his family. Canon Maddy demolished the old rectory and built a new house that still overlooks the church. He furnished it in a grand style with all mod cons, although it's doubtful whether he went to the extremes of one of his colleagues, whose grandiose sideboard was exhibited at the International Exhibition of 1872. The improbably-named Revd W.K.W. Chafy Chafy persuaded a firm in Warwick to make him an enormous cabinet in oak and ebony with shelves edged with purple velvet and embroidered with gold.

Down Hatherley has another, equally well remembered, son. In 1893, Henry and Emily Maddy were shocked when Gladys, their twenty-two-year-old daughter, married Frederick Courtney Selous. Not only was he twice her age, but he was the stuff of *The Boys' Own Paper* as the career he had pursued since the age of nineteen was that of elephant hunter. He lived much of his life within the African Bush, hunting big game with an enormous four-bore muzzle loader. In the 1880s he started work with Cecil Rhodes as a property developer, just as Africa began to open up. Although Selous proved a poor businessman, he became a highly respected explorer and his diaries encouraged a nineteen-year-old Cambridge undergraduate to make the first journey on foot from the Cape to Cairo in 1900. Selous did not go

on record about his wife's family, but the young undergraduate, Ewart Grogan, gives us a hint in his own memoirs of what men like Canon Maddy's son-in-law probably thought about religion. 'The company was rather embarrassed by the Bible-flaunting, prayer-moaning extravaganzas of an evangelical madman… such men should be caged, or at least prevented from running loose among the natives.'

Three years after they had married, the rector's daughter was living in Matabeleland when a native rebellion broke out. They returned home, but Selous soon left to roam the world on expedition. He was back in Africa in 1917, when he was killed in action fighting in the First World War.

There could not be two more different men and yet their names are both synonymous with Down Hatherley; one serving the same parish in this little corner of Gloucestershire for half a century, the other endlessly on the move. But in the adjoining parish, not far from the River Severn, lies buried a man who in his war poetry evokes the different experiences that for each man described home:

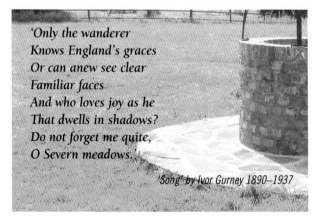

'Only the wanderer
Knows England's graces
Or can anew see clear
Familiar faces
And who loves joy as he
That dwells in shadows?
Do not forget me quite,
O Severn meadows.'

'Song' by Ivor Gurney 1890–1937

FAIRFORD
The Inside Story

'Fairforde never flourished afore the cuming of the Tames unto it and John Tame began the fair new church of Fairford and Edmund Tame finished it.'

John Leland, chronicler, 1540

A parish church in south Gloucestershire has been described as 'the Sistine Chapel of stained glass'. Designed in 1500, its windows took seventeen years to make. But it took twenty years of restoration and half a million pounds raised by Fairford's 200 parishioners for Britain's only complete set of medieval stained glass to be secured for the future.

When the Revd Peter Owen-Jones burst on to BBC2 with his series, *The Battle for Britain's Soul*, it was not long before he was visiting a church in a small town on the southern edge of the Cotswolds. The Parish Church of St Mary the Virgin, Fairford was the perfect backdrop in telling the story of Christianity in medieval England. The colourful Church of England clergyman left the pulpit to use television to help paint a picture of the timeless battle between good and evil. Let loose on our screens were dramatic images of heaven and hell as seen through the medieval church's most potent teaching aid – stained glass. In

King Henry VIII visited Fairford in 1520

a classic 'behind you' moment, Peter Owen-Jones introduced the subject of the final judgment in close-up, with a terrifying red demon peering malevolently over his shoulder from Fairford's great west window.

The Parish Church of St Mary the Virgin, Fairford

Just a few thirteenth-century foundations are all that remain of an old building that was entirely rebuilt in the perpendicular style and consecrated on 20 June 1497 as the 'fair new church'. The fifteenth-century church has survived almost unaltered. Whilst a wealthy local wool-merchant, John Tame, paid for this structure, the crowning glory of Fairford, its stained glass windows, are thought to have been donated by Henry VII, who had been crowned king after he defeated Richard III at the Battle of Bosworth Field in 1485. Henry Tudor went on to dispose of other claimants to the throne from the House of York, and his royal gift of windows for Fairford may well have been an attempt to purge his guilt. It is possible that a small figure in the great west window, which depicts the judgment of heaven and hell, is of the king himself, no doubt hoping for a merciful verdict.

Today's visitors (the wise bring binoculars) can look at hundreds of faces in these windows knowing that glass-painters often drew on family and friends as well as local celebrities to depict both biblical characters and the demons of hell. 'They were having a lot of fun with their work,' says glass conservator, Keith Barley, adding that 'this is the best of the best'.

Unlike most churches today, the twenty-eight windows in St Mary's were designed to be a complete picture of the Christian faith. Look around, and everything that you need to know about the life you must live, if you wish to be saved from hell, is

here. It took seventeen years for the team working in Westminster, which included glaziers and painters from the Netherlands, to make these windows. Led by the king's own glazier, Barnard Flower, they began work on the design drawn up Richard Fox, Bishop of Durham, in 1500.

In August 1520, King Henry VIII came to Fairford and attended mass in the church. It would be fascinating to know, in the light of his subsequent turbulent dealings with the church, what effect these windows had on him. Firstly Henry VIII's agents, then the iconoclasts of the Reformation and finally the weapons of the English Civil War would ensure that the sound of breaking glass would echo through every church for the next 150 years. Amazingly, here not a pane was broken although the west window was blown out in a storm in 1703, and in the 1840s, the glass was touched up as part of a general Victorian restoration of the interior. Nearly 500 years on from Henry VIII's visit, we can enter the church and see how daylight filtering through painted glass brought their faith to life for medieval Christians. As the final window was reinstated recently, the 1703 damage was made good.

A jumble of glass, like a jigsaw without a picture on its box, was revealed to be the 'judgment of David'. Now a new generation in Fairford are learning about the Bible from the windows. 'It's difficult to imagine life without them,' says a member of the choir.

'The Last Judgment' – detail of the great west window in Fairford

had just experienced. The door remained unlocked. We all owe a lot to the Fr Matthews of the world, who keep their churches and their prayers always available to us, the mad, the bad and the sad, as well as for those who just want to have a look around.

I also owe much to the gentleman who was apparently alone, quietly minding his own business, in Fairford Church, when I visited. Although a fine old building outside, St Mary's has to be seen from inside so I was relieved to find the door wide open. Now I could see for myself what has been described as the finest and most complete set of medieval stained glass windows of any parish church in England.

Unfortunately, just as I started to look at the windows, my mobile telephone rang. In the presence of the angels, the patriarchs, the holy family and last, but not least, the devil, I knew that I must make my apologies and leave immediately. It was a few minutes before I could return to look at the figures, feeling rather sheepish at having introduced an element of the twenty-first century into their medieval splendour. My church-watching host, whose presence ensured that Fairford was open today, was waiting anxiously for me. 'Did you see who it was who just rushed out?' he asked with alarm.

'That was me,' I said.

'No, no, I know you!' he said. 'This was a thin man with a phone… where did he come from, where did he go?'

I was still trying and failing to convince him that I exactly fitted the description of a 'thin man with phone', when there was a strange whirring noise in the church. 'What the dickens is that?' he asked, almost jumping out of his skin. At which point, the organ started emitting the familiar notes of Graham Kendrick's worship song 'Shine, Jesus shine'. Now I jumped too,

We are only ever able to visit the nation's favourite churches because of the numbers of volunteers in every community who give up mornings and afternoons to 'church watch'. Many churches now leave the door unlocked from dawn to dusk, an act of faith that has been greatly encouraged in recent times by Andrew Lloyd-Webber's Open Church Trust.

Recently, I came upon a London church on a weekday morning, where Morning Prayer was advertised. However, this church was firmly locked until after the clock had struck the hour for prayers to begin, so I began to think that they were being said behind closed doors (one English Cathedral goes so far as not to open its doors to visitors until the prayers are over). Arriving late and a bit out of breath, Fr Matthew was surprised to be joined by a visitor. We left the church door open and began. After a few moments someone started playing the piano in the church very loudly. We stopped. Fr Matthew asked the pianist, a complete stranger, to stop playing and join us. 'Where is the loo?' demanded the pianist. 'If you haven't got one, I'll kill you.'

The priest dealt with this obvious intimidation with kindness and not a little courage. The pianist decided to leave, and soon we were once again alone, saying our prayers for the troubled world, an example of which we for surely no one else had come in past us?

Somehow they had – 'they' being the youngest child that I have ever seen playing a full size pipe-organ. But there he was, clearly in full and confident charge. 'That's terrific,' I said, through much relief at discovering that the church was not haunted. 'Oh good,' the child said. 'I'll play it again.' And he did, much louder.

I returned to contemplating the stained glass and came face to face with the terrifying red demon in the west window. Immediately, another voice behind me made me jump again, this time a female one and aristocratic in tone. 'If you look closely at the windows, I think that you will see some of us who still live here!'

Was this a statement about the practice of the medieval glass-painters using the faces of parishioners for figures in the windows, for Joseph and Mary, perhaps even for the Devil, and was I supposed now to recognize their descendants? Or was it something more troublingly theological, about the timeless conflict between good and evil? I felt as if I was given my answer through the third and even grander and louder performance of 'Shine, Jesus, shine' that erupted from the organ console. As I left the church, my host was still full of questions, but as suddenly as she had been at my side, the lady with the aristocratic demeanour seemed to vanish into thin air.

There has to be a simple explanation for all these appearances, probably another entrance to this lovely building. But to me it seemed as though I had been transported from a quiet twenty-first century afternoon in a beautiful church into a medieval mystery play. It was as if the figures in the windows had come alive – through the church-watcher, the musician and the mysterious woman – to tell me their stories of mystery, of celebration and of self-recognition. They had given me the inside story on Fairford.

God bless all church-watchers!

'Lord, the light of your love is shining,
in the midst of the darkness, shining:
Jesus, light of the world, shine upon us;
set us free by the truth you now bring us -
shine on me, shine on me.
Shine, Jesus, shine,
fill this land with the Father's glory;
blaze, Spirit, blaze,
set our hearts on fire.
Flow, river, flow,
flood the nations with grace and mercy;
send forth your word, Lord,
and let there be light!'

Graham Kendrick

The Mount of Ascension and the Holy Spirit descends at Pentecost

23
RAMSBURY
A Memory of Angels

'*When I first came to Ramsbury after becoming Bishop of Salisbury in 1993, I was struck by the carved angels on the side of the litany desk, and realised that I had seen them before. Puzzling over this, I mentioned it to my mother, who said that when my father had briefly been curate in Ramsbury, I had often been in the church, and I had always been fascinated by that carving. The next time I came to Ramsbury, I sat on the floor to get a child's eye view of the carving, and suddenly realised that they have stayed in my mind all these years. I cannot have been more than two, as we were only nine months in Ramsbury. I think it must have been my earliest memory of a distinct place.*'

The Right Revd David Stancliffe, quoted in Holy Cross Church: A Guide, History and Meditation *by Barbara Croucher, 2005*

'Is this the nation's best kept secret?' *Songs of Praise* presenter, Diane Louise Jordan, asked when she came here to celebrate Easter in 2000. Like me, she had never heard of this old town under the Marlborough Downs, which before the Norman Conquest had boasted a bishop's palace.

Long before the first Easter of the new millennium, John Kirby, as *Songs of Praise* producer, was given the task of finding a church for the live broadcast. His route to discovering Ramsbury was not straightforward. Peter Hullah, headmaster of Chetham's Grammar School in Manchester, had been an enthusiastic supporter of the city's *Music Live* edition of *Songs of Praise*, letting loose all the talents of his school's famous music tradition, and had agreed to help John.

John Kirby said, 'but then he had gone away to be a Church of England bishop, and he suggested "why don't you come and do something in my new home?" Quite honestly, although I thought I knew the area, I had never heard of Ramsbury.'

Could it be the little gem every producer always dreams of finding? In fact, John's discovery *was* a little gem – but that was the problem. 'I worried at first that it was too small for the cameras, then that it was too big; where were we going to find enough people to fill the church?'

Back in the BBC, John's colleagues hinted unhelpfully that the first Easter service of the new millennium ought to be televised from somewhere that everyone knew. But they need not have worried. On a sunny St George's Day, Holy Cross, Ramsbury wished viewers 'Happy Easter!' from a packed building that John now believes is one of the nation's most prayed-in churches.

The Parish Church of Holy Cross, Ramsbury with Axford, Wiltshire

Holy Cross Church is probably built on the site of an Anglo-Saxon cathedral. From 909 to 1058, this was the headquarters for the successive bishops of Ramsbury. Three bishops went on to become Archbishops of Canterbury. But from 1058 until 1974, when a new suffragan bishop of Ramsbury within the

Diocese of Salisbury was created, Ramsbury was an ecclesiastical backwater. Alas, even John Betjeman does not mention this church in his guide.

The present church was begun in the thirteenth century. A hundred years later, the nave was completed, together with two side chapels and finally the north and south aisles. The Darrell Chapel was finished by 1500. Like so many churches, Holy Cross suffered from all the ravages of English history. At the time of the Reformation, the rood screen and wall paintings were destroyed, and then during the Civil War further damage was done. By 1891, drastic work was required to stop parts of the church from collapsing altogether.

A huge contribution came from a local benefactor, Angela Burdett Coutts, the first woman to be created a baroness in her own right, who also funded many churches in the East End of London. Amongst her gifts were the limed oak choir stalls, which help make the restored chancel one of the best features of Holy Cross. The organ, with its case described by Nikolaus Pevsner as 'a very pretty gothic piece', has some

93

pipework dating from 1778 but has since been rebuilt and enlarged.

I don't think that Daniel Defoe ever visited Ramsbury, but he might well have summed up Holy Cross with the words that he used to describe a stately home in the south of England. 'A good old place, but very ancient, spacious and convenient rather than fine, but exceedingly pleasant by its situation.'

After my father died in 1986, his ashes were scattered on the crest of the downs in southern England. It was not a place that I would have chosen, for the only time I had joined him walking on that same hill, we had had our heads bent against a ferocious winter gale. The wind kidnapped any attempts at conversation, just as his ashes later scattered in a matter of seconds into leafless trees on the ridge.

I had forgotten that it was not only because my father believed we were being 'done good' as we gasped for breath on these marches. We also stopped to look at the view. I grew up stopping to look at the view all over Britain. Even though it was usually after a prolonged physical ordeal, I loved those moments. Before I had a

camera, I would return home to draw my memory of the scene: a distant church, its spire or tower peeping above ancient oaks without their leaves (I found it hard to draw trees in full leaf). Those childhood views were of England at peace under the huge southern sky, one that less than twenty years before, as my father used to remind us, had been full of the angry dogfights of the Battle of Britain. It was right that his ashes flew up into the same sky where some of his best friends had died.

I was thinking of my father as I stood in a field overlooking Ramsbury. My father's own favourite view, not so many miles to the west, was also made by an old village in the bottom of a valley. But trying to photograph Holy Cross, which is concealed by huge old trees in the churchyard, meant an awkward walk across stubble. As I staggered over the field, I remembered that my father rarely took us down into 'the view'. 'Whatever for!' he would ask testily, anticipating crowds and closed tearooms. We never went into a church. If I wanted to join him in worship, I needed to stand in silence with him after a long walk and look at the view.

This hilltop view of Ramsbury is as difficult to

Carved oak angel on the litany desk: a childhood memory for the Bishop of Salisbury

photograph as any on my journey. 'Some things can't be captured – they can only be remembered,' my father used to say. The producer of the Easter service, John Kirby, laughs when I tell him. 'Yes I've been in that field with a camera and on the dangerous bend where the church is briefly visible, but it doesn't do justice to the place.'

Ramsbury may seem to its visitors just another attractive country town, proud as it is of its century, old silver band and with its variety of shops. But some of its inhabitants have turned down work promotions to stay here. And Holy Cross Church also has Barbara Croucher.

The poet Kathleen Raine says that 'the work of the artist is not to reproduce what everybody sees, but to heal our souls; to remind us as it were, of our native country – the world of the spirit – and tell us that it is there all the time'. This is partly what *Songs of Praise* tries to do, so often filmed in stunning landscapes as local people sketch personal stories of their native country, capturing the world of the spirit.

Barbara Croucher was trained as a geographer and then spent twenty years working in publishing. So when she added history to her other formidable skills, producing a guide to her local church, Holy Cross, she was able to create a work of beauty. The book has drawn on the talents of the community working together, including photographer David Stevens who came straight to Holy Cross from an assignment in St Paul's Cathedral, and of other local artists and designers. The result is not just a guide to Holy Cross's history and architecture, it is also a meditation, telling us that the world of the spirit 'is there all the time'.

'"Church" can be confining,' Barbara says, as we talk in the nave. She was doing the flowers when I met her, and began by quietly enthusing about 'Little Fishes', a scheme which helps children aged up to four feel confident enough to be able to push open the church door and explore the building. But her greatest gift is to listen. She finds time to listen when no one else has time.

Before I leave, two people much older than the target age of 'Little Fishes' wrestle with the door and hover briefly nearby. Barbara goes over to them. She is careful not to invade their space but before long, I can tell that she is hearing about a funeral service later in the week for a beloved parent. I can also tell that although they have never met before, Barbara is helping them to make connections, to find 'their native country' by telling them what they really wish to know, answering the questions that funeral directors don't answer. I quickly see why Bishop David Stancliffe has given her the first 'Cross of Aldhelm', his own way of recognizing lay people who make a difference within his diocese.

Travelling on from Ramsbury towards Wales, I remember a Celtic Night Prayer from the Northumbrian Community, which Barbara has included in the church guide to be a comfort to people who may never go into church except for a funeral:

'Be gentle with the one who walks with grief.
If it is you, be gentle with yourself.
Swiftly forgive; walk slowly, pausing often.
Take time, be gentle as you walk with grief.'

24

MORRISTON
Tabernacl

'In their music, they do not sing in unison like the inhabitants of other countries, but in different parts; that in the company of singers, which one very frequently meets with in Wales, you shall hear as many different parts and voices as there are performers, who all at length unite with organic melody in one consonance and soft sweetness.'

Giraldus Cambrensis, twelfth-century historian, describing singing in Wales

Seventy miles to the west of Cardiff is Swansea, once at the centre of the Industrial Revolution. Here stands the most famous building at the heart of the literary, musical and social culture of Wales – the chapel. It has long been a natural home for *Songs of Praise*.

In July 1969, I was lying in hospital feeling sorry for myself. A television near my bedside was intended to prevent me moaning at anyone visiting this grumpy patient. But even the drama and spectacle broadcast live and in colour from Caernarvon Castle of the Queen investing her son as Prince of Wales failed to dispel my misery.

I was still groaning with pain later when *Songs of Praise* came on. It was almost the first time that I had watched the programme, and it literally had me sitting up in bed and beginning to feel better. The television pictures of the Prince of Wales had gone from colour for the investiture to black and white as he progressed from a medieval castle in North Wales to a Victorian chapel in South Wales. But as he walked into this chapel, Tabernacl in Morriston, an enormous congregation were already in full voice. It was the sound that had fascinated the historian, Giraldus, some 800 years before, and which acted as my introduction to the *Cymanfaoedd Canu*, the great Welsh hymn-singing tradition.

The camerawork was crude, with pictures that would not be tolerated by today's *Songs of Praise* directors. But that night, it could not have mattered less. Grainy shots of the congregation singing from the heart drew me easily into their company and to their story of faith. There were children singing without even a glance at their hymn sheets, ranks of men in smart blazers, uniformed nurses in their caps and, as I insist to unbelieving younger producers today, a row of hospital matrons in full fig.

For thirty years, every time I directed *Songs of Praise*, I hoped to recapture that experience but without ever quite managing it. Watching it again, compared with a beautiful new *Songs of Praise* made in the chapel in 2004, it does look very rough, and yet the power of the thing is almost better now than I remember from my first viewing.

That programme still sends my spirits soaring. There is no presenter except the minister of the time, the Revd W.A. Davies, and he speaks in Welsh. But the translator tells us enough: the second hymn describing 'the angelic hosts above and the church below uniting to sing God's praise'. And what a sound follows. 'I doubt His Royal Highness has ever heard eight such crack choirs leading the singing,' says the commentary.

Memory has not played a trick on me either, for there in the balcony, unmistakably, are a row of hospital matrons. No wonder that I sat up in bed and pulled myself together.

Tabernacl Independent Congregational Chapel, Morriston, Swansea

In 1872, three men came together to work on the most spectacular chapel to be built in South Wales. The immense auditorium built in the shadow of a huge spire would later be described as 'the climax of non-conformist triumphal'. The minister, William Emlyn Jones, the builder, Daniel Edwards, and the architect, John Humphrey, created what a local paper called 'an oasis in the midst of unsightly works and manufactories'.

It drew on a mixture of all the architectural styles that appealed to the three men. The huge classical columns at the entrance were so popular that the architect used this feature for three other chapels. For once, all four exterior walls were built to the same high standard (often only the main street frontage was properly finished and decorated).

Inside, the auditorium is surrounded by a gallery on all sides held up by elegant cast-iron columns, its front edge rising and falling in graceful curves. The only purpose for any chapel was to provide seating for as many people as possible to see and hear the preacher in the pulpit, but Tabernacl also has seating behind the pulpit for a large choir.

This pulpit of richly carved mahogany is itself a huge space. In the 1969 Songs of Praise programme, it comfortably held three ministers. By contrast, the communion table is small and almost insignificant. On each side huge plain windows were positioned to let in as much natural light as possible. Recently, stained glass has been inserted in the windows on either side of the organ, whose vast pipes dominate even the huge and ornate pulpit.

Huw Tregelles Williams at the console of the Hill and Co and Norman and Beard organ

Tabernacl is a Grade I listed building and almost one million pounds has been given by Welsh Heritage and by charitable trusts to help a small independent congregation keep the building intact.

My journey to Tabernacl is a journey into another language. Going west into Wales, the station loudspeaker no longer announces 'Bridgend' but 'Pen-y-bont', and finally 'Abertawe', Welsh for Swansea, once home of the poet Dylan Thomas. The train travelling into the land of song today is not filled with the sounds of poetry or hymn-singing, however, but the din of ringtones as a gaggle of young girls compete to show off their new mobile telephones. Our arrival at Abertawe is accompanied by a dalek-like version of 'Land of my Fathers' which produces the loudest of shrieks.

The station taxi driver, curious to know why I am going to church on a Saturday, recognizes my destination. 'No, I've never been in the door, but of course,' and his voice changes to a tone of reverence, 'it is the place where the Morriston choir exercises its privilege to sing.'

Entering the huge building by a tiny side door, two further small doors lead out of a dark lobby; one displays a faded notice in Welsh, the other leads into a broom cupboard. Someone once described the purpose of these places – 5,000 chapels were built in Wales in just 100 years – as 'a door to understanding through a door of emotion'. At last I enter the auditorium of Tabernacl where, in 1969, the young Prince of Wales came to hear his subjects 'exercising their privilege to sing'.

Huw Tregelles Williams regularly conducts *Songs of Praise* from Wales, and as a former head of music for BBC Wales, also conducts the Morriston Male Voice Choir. He plays the organ for the Sunday service in Tabernacl. 'I feel comfortable when the chapel is full,' he says, 'for then it's got meaning.' Sadly, on most Sundays, the chapel is far from full. Up to forty people sit scattered around where once the nurses and matrons assembled in a packed auditorium.

'The last minister left on Easter Day,' Huw Tregelles tells me as he opens up the organ, 'and now the search is on for a Welsh-speaker to occupy the pulpit. But you have to ask, who now wants to listen to a sermon for half an hour?'

Well, at least some still do. The small congregation of Tabernacl may be aging, and the leadership of the chapel may mostly be in the hands of people in their eighties, but they are a remarkably faithful remnant. John Thomas, clerk of the works and lover of all things mechanical, has played a huge part in the restoration of the building. His personal touches include a subtly concealed rail under the piano, allowing it to be moved for recitals.

The history of the organ in Tabernacl tells the story of change and decay. It arrived in 1922 from the builders Hill and Co and Norman and Beard. 'It was just as the two firms came together, even to the extent that the left-hand side of the keyboard and the stops are pure Hill and Co,' Huw Tregelles says as he demonstrates the versatility of the three-manual instrument. Even more significantly, the organ arrived when South Wales was still grieving for its war dead. The First World War had put an end to the great revivals and the authority of chapel pulpits. The organ would soon support not only worship but secular concerts. The great days seemed over.

There are still great days at Tabernacl, but the ministry of music has replaced the preacher. International stars like Peter Dawson have come to sing Bach, Handel and Verdi. It was here that W. Penfro Rowlands, chorus master at the chapel and the composer of the famous hymn-tune 'Blaenwern', conducted 'Hiawatha's Wedding Feast', a very popular oratorio before the Second World War, in the presence of the composer, Coleridge Taylor. Right up at the back of the gallery, I look at a tiny pew and wonder how many years it has been since it was last occupied. 'Oh, I can tell you the exact date,' says Huw. 'It was the night Bryn Terfel was here for a charity concert. The event sold out in minutes and you could not get a seat for love nor money.'

No longer, in the words of the late historian Glanmor Williams, 'is there any latter-day Elijah to be discerned on any mountain top, charged with a prophetic charisma that once more might invoke the celestial lightning flash.' Yet once in 1969, watching *Songs of Praise* from Tabernacl, I was led 'through a door of emotion to a door of understanding'. I would go on to become a religious broadcaster, and to film the very first interviews for the programme where local people would trace, as they still do today, their own unique stories of faith.

Music is a draw to Tabernacl today, regardless of language

'... there I felt the dread of damnation and the joy of forgiveness. My ambition was first aroused there, and my pride laid low by having it enforced on me that I was wholly without merit – every thought and feeling of greater profundity than the course of daily living, human and divine, direct me back to that old grey chapel.'

Sir Owen Edwards

25
BODMIN
Petroc

'*But somewhere, somewhere underneath
    the dunes
Somewhere among the cairns or in the caves
The Celtic saints would come to me, the ledge
Of time we walk on, like a thin cliff-path
High in the mist would show the precipice.*'

John Betjeman

Some time around the year AD 600, a monk arrived at the mouth of the River Camel on Cornwall's north coast. Some believe that he came from Ireland but others that this son of a Welsh prince hailed from South Wales. He was to found a priory in Bodmin, close to what was later to become the site of Cornwall's largest parish church.

Fourteen hundred years later, Pamela – a listener to BBC Radio Cornwall – moved to Bodmin after forty happy years spent in Kent. 'The loneliness I felt at leaving my friends has been offset by the friendship and kindness of St Petroc's, Bodmin. I thank God that I found this, my favourite church.'

When John Betjeman died in 1984, he was living just yards from the point where Petroc came ashore. Trebetherick was a place of childhood holiday memories for the lonely only child. His biographer, Bevis Hillier, says that 'Cornwall was Betjeman's Holy Well'. Here is the source then for his 'wistful yearning for old and warm times'. And it was here 'from violent family arguments and pools of bruised silence he fled, and sought forgiveness in remote damp-walled churches which echoed to the clattering of bats and the ticking of beetles'.

For a short time, I went with John Betjeman into such buildings. With his characteristic stumbling gait,

he usually managed to pull out an obscure guide from the ancient raffia bag that went with him everywhere and then began a rapid inspection, making no attempt to watch his feet on the uneven floor. Following in his wake, I tripped a few times myself, distracted and entranced by the rich flow of information that Betjeman gleaned as he looked around, not just about the architecture but about the clues that generations of worshippers had left behind in the church.

His *Pocket Guide to English Parish Churches* is full of first impressions. Indeed, John Betjeman's own grave lies 'in the middle of a golf course' under the lea of 'the crooked spire of St Enodoc', close also to Petroc's landing place and, just as his guide tells us, the 'restored interior is dark and ancient'.

A few miles to the south is St Petroc's, Bodmin, where, the guide says, 'though much furbished up in Victorian times, it retains its old wagon roofs'. 'Furbished' is a word that perfectly describes the work of well-meaning nineteenth-century benefactors whose work we see today in so many of the nation's favourite churches.

Sir John Betjeman and Sir Charles Tennyson await their cue in a BBC film in 1968

The Parish Church of Saint Petroc's, Bodmin

Even before St Petroc came to Bodmin in AD 530, a hermit called St Guron was already here. Before he died in 564, Petroc made Bodmin 'the abode of the Monks' and had founded his priory there. There were other early churches around the site, and some of the stonework in the tower of St Petroc's is Norman.

The present church was built between 1469 and 1472. The whole town contributed to the cost, which in present day money would have been about half a million pounds; the vicar donated a year's pay to help. The church is built with local Bodmin stone in Cornish Perpendicular. It is 151 feet long and 65 feet wide. For once, John Betjeman was wrong when he wrote 'it retains its old wagon roofs' as the present wagon roof is a restoration, made after the spire was struck by lightning in 1699 and fell through into the church.

There is a nice story about Bodmin's bell. On 29 August 1743, John Wesley had got completely lost on Bodmin moor. Even today, crossing the moor in anything other than bright sunlight, the traveller is nervous of sudden mists. Wesley travelled up to seventy miles a day on horseback, often fitting in preaching on the way, so it's likely that he will have been exhausted too. But after getting lost, he then heard the bell tolling and managed to reach safety. This may have been the time when Wesley travelled through heavy rain to preach in Bodmin town hall. He came every summer for thirty-one years to Cornwall, but he was not always welcome. One rector wrote of his preaching, 'it is not guarded; it is dangerous; it may lead people into enthusiasm.'

In the wide south aisle a Byzantine casket is on view, containing the remains of the saint, on display, but now protected as securely as the crown jewels. The casket has been stolen three times, the first in 1176, the last as recently as 1994, when it was eventually found – to everyone's relief – in

'A grand Norman font of local type': John Betjeman

a field in Yorkshire. Local people had been devastated by the theft. It is one of the Duchy of Cornwall's most treasured possessions and has been described as 'representing the spirit of everything Cornish'.

All of the stained glass is Victorian. Unusually, an 1824 east window was replaced in 1896, but, as one guide tells visitors, 'modernisers have ever been busy in Bodmin'. But that can sometimes reap benefits – a beautifully preserved nineteenth-century reredos, for example, has recently been uncovered behind the 1932 wooden replacement.

There are two ancient items in the church: a Norman font, supported on pillars decorated with angels, and the St Petroc's lectern, made up of bits of medieval misericord. There is a mystery behind this, but one that the visitor must look closely at to discover. The carved wooden figure's hand, holding up the lectern, has five fingers and a thumb. Was this a mistake or was he a monk with a difference, from Bodmin's forgotten past?

I don't know whether one of Cornwall's busiest roundabouts was then so close to the county's biggest parish church when John Betjeman came to visit. Today the traffic is moving so fast that I have to make three circuits before I can read the inviting notice, 'The Church is open'. Just beyond this notice there is an empty little side road, offering an invitation to park that seems too good to be true. It is. The road, perhaps Bodmin's version of the apple in the Garden of Eden, leads to the police station.

But apart from a brief struggle with parking, there are no more disappointments in my visit to St Petroc's. The grand prix style roundabout, however, might explain why the present vicar's wife does not think that *Songs of Praise* has ever been to this very fine church. Many a priest and organist began a recording in ill-humour when they discovered that the BBC needed to park six large vans outside the door – simply impossible here. Fortunately new technology now allows a small crew to arrive on foot with large suitcases. So there is hope yet that the people of St Petroc's will be given an opportunity to tell their story on BBC1.

Pamela, who had nominated this church, is waiting for me in the sun-filled south aisle, and introduces me to Dorothy and Bill, two of the stalwarts who do 'church-watching'. Their friendly welcome to the church book and gift store doesn't fully describe the need for their presence, however. Not only have the relics of Saint Petroc been stolen, but as recently as 2001, ninety-five pieces of beautiful stained glass were smashed.

Dorothy and Bill introduce me to a Cornish speciality, 'star gazy pie', a pasty filled with fish, and tells me about a local scheme that not only feeds hungry stomachs but also helps people in Peru. It is based on 'the plastic duck race', in which competitors sponsor their own plastic duck to float down a stream. The money pays for women in Peru to be given a real duck, which will help keep a family fed while building up their own home economy. St Petroc, 'a cheerful giver, burning with ceaseless charity', would have approved.

I think he would have approved also of the annual mammoth fund-raising event in the church called 'the Christmas tree fair'. This takes a familiar winter feature to extremes. 'Well, there are usually 100 decorated trees – at least!' says the vicar's wife, Jane, laughing as she describes an event which is drawing visitors from far and wide. It must look like a scene from Macbeth, when 'Birnam Wood to high Dunsinane hill shall come'.

If 'star gazy pie', plastic duck racing and the great Christmas tree invasion are all part of Cornish life today, so is hymn singing. Pamela tells me, 'We have a choir trainer who gets the whole congregation to sing. My way of learning new hymns is to start by saying no, and to end up singing them around the house!'

I have only just managed, through the encyclopedic knowledge of Canon Rex Hurrell, who once served in the diocese, to trace the words of a Cornish hymn that I remember being sung set to Henry Purcell's tune 'Westminster Abbey' on *Songs of Praise* in 1978, from a huge Methodist chapel in Redruth, Cornwall. I will also never forget hearing it sung again in a spontaneous performance in a Redruth pub!

'All these Cornish shores are holy,
Here the Saints in prayer did dwell,
Raising font and altar lowly
Preaching far with staff and bell –
Piran, Petroc, Paul Aurelian,
Euny, Samson, Winwaloe.'

Canon Miles Brown, one-time vicar of St Winnow and St Veep

26

OTTERY ST MARY
Genius and Generosity

*'**a**nd as oft*
with unclosed lids, already had I dreamt
of my sweet birth-place, and the old
church-tower,
whose bells, the poor man's only music, rang
from morn to evening, all the hot fair-day,
so sweetly, that they stirred and haunted me
with a wild pleasure, falling on mine ear
most like articulate sounds of things to come!
So gazed I, till the soothing things I dreamt
lulled me to sleep, and sleep prolonged my
dreams!'

from 'Frost at Midnight' by Samuel Taylor Coleridge 1772–1834

Travelling east from Cornwall into Devon, we come to the birthplace of Samuel Taylor Coleridge, born in the shadow of a church which the poet immortalized in the poem above describing his daydream during a dull lesson in school.

When John de Grandisson died on 16 July 1369, his bequests included one that would seem strange today: a lectern, in the form of a huge carved eagle. Painted bright red, probably the same colour as when it was made in 1342, the eagle lectern is still used today every time the Bible is read in the lady chapel of St Mary's. The parish church itself was another gift to the town from a man who described himself as an 'unworthy and unprofitable servant'. In fact, Bishop John de Grandisson's spiritual influence extended well beyond his own Diocese of Exeter, then even larger than today, and included the whole of Cornwall.

For forty-one years, Bishop John de Grandisson faithfully served his diocese, rarely leaving it, unlike many of his fellow bishops and clergy. Robert Sumpter, Dean of Exeter Cathedral, lived in London and spent his time 'hunting and hawking'. A number of local vicars were described as 'missing'. The rector of another Devon parish was also rector of a parish far away in Wales.

These were troubled and dangerous times. In 1343, when the bishop was preaching in one of his churches, he was attacked by a mob armed with bows and arrows intent on killing him. Five years later, the 'Black Death' plague struck Ottery and seven of the priests from St Mary's died.

Bishop John de Grandisson is still remembered every year when the people of the diocese sing Christmas carols in Exeter Cathedral at a special service bearing his name. He loved the seasons of Advent and Lent and observed all the saints' days and many of the saints in the much-loved 1662 *Book of Common Prayer* are there because they were first included in John de Grandisson's own liturgical prayers.

Although he was often given to 'harsh and violent language', I think that we can understand why. For a man who cared deeply about worship, he had to deal with choirs who 'giggled and laughed through services'. Often they quarrelled in the choir stalls and played tricks such as pouring hot candle wax on to the heads of members of the congregation seated in front of them. There was apparently 'much noise and laughter' during services in Ottery St Mary.

The ultimate sanction for the bishop was to 'excommunicate' malefactors, but such an extreme response, involving the 'dashing of candles to the ground and the ringing of bells' and the barring from holy communion of the sinner, was rare. Even today, there can be 'off days' for cathedral choirs, and giggling is not unknown. I did wonder recently whether ecclesiastical 'ASBOs' should be introduced, as when attending evensong at an English cathedral, one of the gentlemen of the choir consumed a slice of cake between each sung response.

The former Collegiate Church of Saint Mary of Ottery, Ottery St Mary, Devon

Bishop John de Grandisson supervised the completion of his own cathedral, which was only half built when he was made a bishop in 1327. England was still then under the authority of the Pope, and so John was consecrated Bishop of Exeter in Avignon, where the Papal Court was then based. Bishop John began to establish his own spiritual authority in England and founded a collegiate church in Ottery St Mary in 1337. Although only half its length, the design of the church was modelled on Exeter Cathedral.

It stands on the northern edge of quite a small town where the first church on the site was consecrated in 1257. Bishop Grandisson's building was a reconstruction of that church with new twin towers built on the existing structure. Internally, it is like a very small cathedral in a cruciform shape. The north aisle is almost a separate church; known as the Dorset aisle, it was added in 1520 and has a beautiful fan-vaulted stone roof.

Beyond the altar screen is a cosy lady chapel containing the bishop's gilded red wooden eagle lectern, and many other items in the church survive from his time, including the astronomical clock in the south aisle (there is a similar clock in Exeter Cathedral). In 1545, when Henry VIII dissolved the College of Priests, St Mary's possessed ninety-nine copes and twenty-five full sets of vestments as well as three solid gold chalices.

There were three organs in the medieval church, including one in the lady chapel and one on the rood loft. The present organ, built by London builders Flight and Robson, began life in 1828 in the west gallery. It was moved in 1901 into the choir and divided in two. Described by an enthusiast as 'a two-manual organ that thinks it is a four-manual instrument', the 'little giant' is now in the expert care of Ottery's organist, Michael Farley, who is also an organ builder.

In 1850, the architect Butterfield was employed to undertake what the Victorians called restoration. The church must have been in good shape when he arrived as there is very

little of the heavy-handed 'improvement' seen in so many other churches. Although Butterfield's marble font, a real eye-catcher with its vivid decoration, did not gain his approval, John Betjeman describes St Mary's as a 'grand town church'.

Like so many churches, St Mary's has its own website, where I began my visit. Simon Franklin, writing the introduction as team rector, is very welcoming, saying 'by entering it you touch part of the church. And though we may not know each other, you will be prayed for, as we do each week for all who visit the church.'

When *Songs of Praise* came from Ottery St Mary for Harvest, the programme drew on the surrounding communities of rural Devon. Included was the story of Peter and Maggie Whiteman, from Cullompton, who described to Jonathan Edwards their project of harvesting pieces of wood that no one else wants. 'Much as God shapes our blemished personalities and shapes it into his character, we are trying to use all the natural resources of his creation.'

Near St Mary's, in St Andrew's, Cullompton, there is a huge carved beam that looks like a piece of discarded blemished wood but is unique, an ancient relic in another church from Bishop Grandisson's time. As the Whiteman family's unusual approach to harvest reminded me of this strange object, it gave me the excuse for a diversion on the way to Ottery.

Visiting St Andrew's in its Monday-morning emptiness, it is a shock to be confronted by a realistic skull. Until the sixteenth century and the Reformation, both St Mary's in Ottery and St Andrew's in Cullompton had a rood loft over the entrance to the chancel, and the

life sized figure of Christ on the cross would have slotted onto this great carved beam called a 'Golgotha', or the 'place of the skull'. At the foot of the cross lay the skull, symbolizing the fall of Adam.

In an age when most people could not read, the preacher would have pointed to the cross and to this skull as he told the story of the fall and of redemption, illustrating the verse in the first letter of Paul to the Corinthians, 'As in Adam all die, so in Christ all will be brought to life.'

It is a powerful image. I am glad to have seen the only remaining Golgotha in England for myself, but if you are of a nervous disposition, you should visit with a friend. After visiting, imagine what a dramatic part it would have played at services when you then visit Ottery St Mary. Four hundred and fifty years later, television cameras still show that a single image can be as effective as many words. In Ottery St Mary, as so often on *Songs of Praise*, there were many moving stories of human life experience, offering personal 'glimpses of God'. But above all, a close-up of someone singing from the heart showed us in a single picture what faith is all about.

'Beauty for brokenness, hope for despair,
Lord, in the suffering, this is our prayer.
Bread for the children, justice, love, peace,
Sunrise to sunset your kingdom increase.
God of the poor, friend of the weak,
Give us compassion, we pray,
Melt our cold hearts,
Let tears fall like rain.
Come change our love
From a spark to a flame.'

Graham Kendrick

27

BRIGHTON
'Blessed Bartholomew'

'In the noise and glitter of cheerful Brighton, this great church is a tall sanctuary of peace. Its interior awes beholders to silence.'

John Betjeman

Our journey continues along the south coast to 'Sussex by the Sea' and Brighton, to find the parish church with the tallest nave in Britain, a huge building that is still unfinished.

For the late Poet-Laureate, Sir John Betjeman, one church more than any other combined his two passions for Victorian architecture and Edwardian railways. Coming to St Bartholomew's was for him to experience the glories of 'London, Brighton and South Coast Railway Religion'. The pilgrimage began at Victoria Station in London where 'The Brighton Belle' was ready with hot-buttered toast and a pot of tea at every seat in the Pullman car. Just as tea was over, the train would pull in under Brighton's ornate iron roof, and those who knew where to look could catch a fleeting glimpse of an enormous brick building towering over nineteenth-century terraced streets, with seagulls wheeling around its high roof. So many made their way to worship in Brighton this way that the services were advertised in newspapers with the footnote: 'fast trains from London'.

High mass to celebrate its Patronal Festival begins with an extraordinary hymn that everyone in church seems to know except me:

'Holy and Mighty, Father, God Supernal,
In this our Festal grant Thy Benediction,
While with glad voices this our Patron's glory
Duly we render.'

Hymn to St Bartholomew

Faithful to the Betjeman experience, I arrive in Brighton by train on a summer's Saturday evening, as punctual as 'The Brighton Belle'. Around the station are busy pavement cafés and many small shops, selling exotic clothes, herbal remedies and revolutionary books, that show no sign of closing even after six o'clock. Only an elderly man with a battered suitcase is going my way. We both turn a corner and there, acting as a backdrop to the end of the little street, is what looks like the tallest brick building in the world, with a small stone cross perched at its top. We are on our way to celebrate

high mass on the feast day of the apostle and saint Bartholomew.

*'Now his devotion urge our faltering footsteps,
His prayers assist us, his example guide us,
Till the same Way, The Truth, the Life in Jesus
We too have chosen.'*

The Parish Church of St Bartholomew's, Brighton

St Bartholomew's has been described as a very large brick shed. Inside it is just one huge open space, its walls 170 feet long, 144 feet high and internally buttressed, the reason why the church, with only its external walls to prop it up, is safe to enter.

It was built in an Italianate style by Edmund Scott, who used little more than different-coloured brick to ornament the interior of the original church. The foundation stone was laid in February 1872 and a little over two years later, the first services were held. At a time when pew rentals excluded the poor from worship, St Bartholomew's was free and open to all through the generosity of an Anglican priest, Arthur Wagner.

Fr Wagner, himself the son of a clergyman, was born in 1824 and studied mathematics at Cambridge University but in 1850 was ordained. Although wealthy, he lived a simple life and was reticent about his generosity, giving £18,000 to build St Bartholomew's as well as four other churches in Sussex. Hearing their curate preach, one parishioner said, 'You would have thought from the way he spoke that he might have contributed a £5 note to the building.' One story about Fr Wagner characterizes the man. When the people who rented homes in the street in which the church stood complained that the new building was so tall that it caused down draughts in their chimneys to blow out their fires, Arthur Wagner bought the houses and reduced their rents.

In 1895, a second phase in the life of the church began. Fr Arthur Cocks was a flamboyant priest who attracted huge congregations. A symphony orchestra played at services and the vicar was led in by a Japanese verger who had once worked in the stables of the Mikado. To match the ornate splendour of the new services, a man described as an 'ecclesiastical stage designer' began to transform the interior. Henry Wilson, who later became a jewellery designer, made the silver-plated altar

frontal which is now in the lady chapel. In 1899, his forty-five-foot high Baldacchino in a Byzantine style was completed, so that the high altar was under a ceiling of gold and mother of pearl.

In 1911, even Wilson's flamboyance was superseded when Italian workers completed the mosaic angels designed by F. Hamilton Jackson placed on either side of the altar. The huge figures of Michael and Raphael, Uriel and Gabriel still watch over worshippers as they come forward for communion. But St Bartholomew's could have been even more exotic. In 1924, 100 years after Father Arthur Wagner's birth, Sir Giles Gilbert Scott, architect of Liverpool Cathedral, came up with a plan to build a huge lady chapel beyond the altar, which would offer worshippers a 'distant prospect of medieval Italy'. But in the same year, the massive roof needed re-slating. Years of struggle to find the funds to support such a unique structure lay ahead.

'A window into beauty' was how the Revd Eddie Neale described St Bartholomew's in his sermon. Eddie used to present religious programmes for BBC Radio Merseyside, so I had not expected to see him in Brighton and was especially surprised to find an evangelical who had been converted at a Billy Graham rally preaching in such a bastion of high Anglo-Catholicism. But as he went on to tell all of us who had come to the solemn high mass for the apostle, 'Jesus said we must be born again and again and again. And in that process I have been learning to love aspects of Catholic worship and spirituality.'

Eddie paid tribute to nineteenth-century priests like Arthur Wagner, who endured persecution and danger simply by placing lighted candles on the altar. 'They built amazing buildings like this to give people a glimpse of heaven in the middle of their slums. They also built night shelters, Sunday schools and hospices. Sometimes these lonely, aristocratic Victorian men became broken in the process, but out of their brokenness they too found salvation and learned to be loved, and they can be seen in faded old photographs cradling the urchins of their parishes and caring for their flock and becoming much-loved saints.'

Today, St Bartholomew's is significantly less well off than the people who live around it, and the building is feeling its age. And yet it attracts much love and voluntary labour from those who belong to it, as well as the huge interest of tourists from around the world.

Fortunately it is now in the care of Fr Vickery House who understands the correct way to use the building about which Betjeman had encouraged the rumour that the clergy processed in on elephants.

By the time the solemn high mass began, Fr 'Vic' had choreographed the unique St Bartholomew's experience. The man with the battered suitcase whom I had followed into the church was followed in by a steady stream of priests who were all greeted by Fr Vickery, but with no sign of a vestry, all seemed to just melt away into the vast space. Meanwhile, a choir and orchestra were rehearsing Haydn's 'Paukenmesse', conducted from the organ by another evident star of St Bartholomew's, Derek Barnes. He and his musicians high up in the west gallery, designed to accommodate 150 performers, were also invisible to the waiting congregation. For this service, Derek had eighteen singers and eighteen musicians, all so perfectly tuned even in rehearsal that I felt ashamed and amazed that the church had never made *Songs of Praise*. Sixty miles away in London, similar performances were filling the Royal Albert Hall for the BBC Proms.

Yet the church was not full when a bell rang and we stood up and started to sing Bartholomew's hymn. And where were the clergy? Quite unexpectedly, an enormous procession suddenly appeared to come through the wall behind the high altar; following a cross, candles and banners, the black-suited clergy now wearing red cassocks had been transformed into a scene from grand opera or *Alice in Wonderland*.

In Fr Wagner's day, such a procession in a church lit by hundreds of candles would have attracted sectarian violence. But Pope Benedict XVI has not sent an army to St Bartholomew's to invade and convert England. Instead, we are in just another Church of England parish church, where all are welcome.

There was no better example of this for me, someone who once found such services baffling and excluding, than the moment when I went up with the musicians to the altar rail to receive communion. This is a well rehearsed routine at St Bartholomew's, but usually without me, the unexpected guest in the gallery. For a

moment it looked as if there would be no room for me to join them and kneel down, but in a spontaneous shuffle, the whole choir made space for the stranger. I felt immediately blessed by their welcome.

As I was kneeling in the space the musicians had made for me, the mystery of how the clergy had appeared out of the wall was solved. When Edward Wilson designed the Baldacchino in 1899, he had concealed the vestry behind the altar, so that the congregation would imagine that the clergy were emerging from the very gates of heaven.

I was to be thankful for the moment when there was 'room for one more' when I was later writing about St Bartholomew's, flying over the Australian desert. Suddenly the jet hit turbulence and we swayed and bumped wildly. Trying to overcome fear by staring fixedly at my notes, I found myself looking at something Fr 'Vic' had said. 'Our Lord is present in the blessed sacrament. It is his presence that guides, directs, sustains and encourages us. His presence in time and space leads us to the eternal truths beyond history and beyond matter.'

From the swaying jet, I travelled back across time and space to St Bartholomew's and to my companions sharing the bread and the wine that night. It was 'food for thought' as an elderly woman rather mysteriously muttered as we returned from the altar, before we all headed out into the Brighton streets under a firework-filled sky.

I might have been writing my last words in another wilder sky, but with St Bartholomew's help, I was ready.

The railway clock in Brighton station

> '*Golden Bartholomew, star-like in glory,*
> *On earth found guileless, Israel's name*
> *adorning;*
> *Aid us thy children, that in light resplendent*
> *We may find portion.*'

28
GOUDHURST
Our Little City Upon the Hill

*'**W**hen church is famed in story of olden
smuggling day
When from the tower the village brought the
foe to bay'*

'Goudhurst' by Mabel Ryan

On one of the highest points of the High Weald of Kent stands an ancient parish church. Its tower offers panoramic views across the 'Garden of England', and the church, which has been open daily to visitors since 1912, looks as if it has slumbered peacefully through the centuries. But it has a different story to tell.

On the afternoon of 21 April 1747, gunshots rang out in anger from the top of the tower of St Mary's, at the centre of the village of Goudhurst. George Kingsmill and Barnet Wollett fell dead in the churchyard below. In that moment, the courageous people of the village together with a handful of dragoons brought an end to a ruthless band of smugglers, known as the Hawkhurst Gang. Named after another village nearby, these smugglers had terrorized local people for years, as they played cat and mouse with the revenue men across much of the south coast of England. Kingsmill, leader of the gang, who had boasted that he had killed fifty customs officers already,

The Bedgebury chapel

111

had given notice that he intended to 'take possession, murder the inhabitants and burn the village down', leaving the villagers no option but to fight back. Some time later, the gang, armed and stripped to the waist, rode across the churchyard to the top of the village, but their bluff was called from the church tower.

Justice and retribution for the surviving gang members was as swift as the skirmish. After his execution, the body of one smuggler was brought from London and suspended in chains on a gibbet outside the village. As recently as the 1980s, a nearby resident believed that the spot was haunted, but visitors today are sometimes disappointed to learn that the deep cuts in the stone by the west door of the church are where ordinary household knives – not swords – were sharpened, and that a skull and crossbones on a tombstone is merely a mason's mark for mortality.

The peaceful visitor who today clambers up the seventy-eight steep steps inside the tower is able to see what a strong defensive position it provided. Looking out over the stone parapet, not only is the whole churchyard and village visible, but also the hop gardens and orchards of the Weald for miles around. But perhaps it was memories of the 1747 skirmish fought from the house of God that prompted the vicar during the Second World War, while the Battle of Britain raged overhead, to forbid the men of the Goudhurst Home Guard to have bullets in their rifles when watching from the tower for enemy invaders.

Wooden effigy of Sir Alexander and Dame Constance Culpeper

The Parish Church of St Mary the Virgin, Goudhurst

The oldest part of the church is in the south-east corner. In the floor of the Bedgebury Chapel are some twelfth-century tiles, which belonged to the church, founded by Robert de Crevecour in 1170. The south aisle roughly forms the length of the church, which until the time of Henry VIII, was where mass was celebrated by monks who walked over from Combwell Priory. By the end of the sixteenth century, the present nave and the north aisle were built, with much of the yellow sandstone being quarried nearby from what is now a pond. Combwell Priory was soon closed, but Goudhurst became a prosperous weaving community.

In 1637, the church tower was struck by lightning and fell down. When it was rebuilt in 1642, it was in an entirely different style to the rest of the building, with a striking west window, similar to the one in the City of London church of St Katharine Cree. The money was raised in London by a public collection called a 'brief', like a street 'flag day'.

In the 1750s, a west gallery for musicians was constructed, and a tombstone in the centre aisle marks the front of this gallery with a monument to the churchwarden who paid the builders after church funds had run out. But by the 1860s, the church had become dilapidated, with the south aisle about to collapse, and a tree growing through the wall. The whole church was then restored, the bespoke musicians' gallery removed and a pipe organ installed.

In the south aisle is one of only forty wooden effigies left in Britain. It depicts the recumbent figures of Sir Alexander Culpeper and his wife, Dame Constance, who died in 1537. Culpeper did not approve of the reformers' plans to strip the medieval church and, when the rood loft was torn down, claimed some of it as his own personal property, and so it survived. His son, also named Alexander, and other family members, are commemorated in a huge memorial showing husband, wife and a line of children kneeling in prayer. By the time of his death in 1599, Culpeper was an ironmaster in the industry that was replacing weaving in the Weald of Kent with the manufacture of cannons for the powerful Elizabethan navy.

When the Songs of Praise cameras arrived in the 1990s, I had moved away from the village that for ten years had

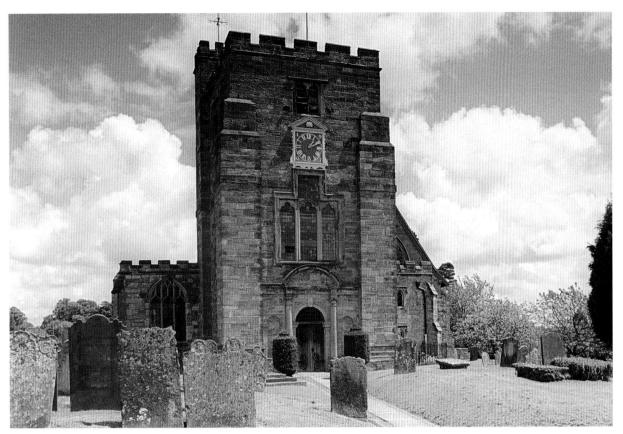

been my home, and now watched the service through the eyes of a BBC friend, the director Simon Hammond. I was relieved and happy to find that he allowed the church, the village and its people the right to self-expression in a way that was completely accurate. All TV producers ought to have this experience, to help paint a story of another community truthfully, as it can be painful to see a familiar place portrayed in ways that are unfamiliar.

It was by no means rare for the whole village to come together to sing. In 1935, St Mary's church had a large choir and the village a 'prize brass band'. To mark the Jubilee of King George V, they all assembled around the tower from which the village had been so well defended in 1747, and sang 'Abide with me'. It was 'Goudhurst en masse', wrote the Revd Harold South. 'The noblest thoughts have filled our minds to make our little city upon the hill which cannot be hid live up to its fine traditions.'

But by the 1980s, only a small number of talented and dedicated singers remained, accompanied by the choir mistress Elizabeth, who protested that she was a pianist rather than an organist. But, from nowhere, the vicar was approached by a musician new to the community, who was to give more than twenty years, service to the church. Cyril Russell, a music teacher, had once held the glamorous position of city organist in Malaga in Spain. His arrival in Goudhurst was like manna from heaven.

Every Saturday morning, Cyril conducted choir practice. Seated at a small upright piano, his method of getting results involved much laughter. He used the great comedian-musician Victor Borge's trick of placing his hands on the keyboard but repeatedly interrupting his playing with a mixture of stories and jokes. He was following in the tradition set by Sydney Nicholson, who founded the School of English Church Music in 1932, now the Royal School of Church Music (RSCM).

'Get the choir to smile whilst singing – there must be no frowning,' was one of Nicholson's principles for good voice production. He invented exercises to produce good articulation like, 'Doleful Dick of Delhi dallies daily at the

door; Philip full of fury finds him flat upon the floor.'
Said and then sung at an ever faster tempo, it was a way
of warming up on a cold wintry morning. Nicholson's
aim was to encourage every village church choir to sing
to the highest possible standard, and thanks to Cyril,
some of Goudhurst's choristers now proudly wear RSCM
medals.

Cyril once told me that he would like to burn a new
hymnbook, but that was the only unkind thing I ever
heard him say. Sunday mornings invariably went without
any displays of musical temperament, even when the
vicar announced the wrong hymn. Cyril remained out of
sight at the console, but the choir facing the
congregation, with not a frown to be seen, helped
transform our worship.

When *Songs of Praise* came to the village, Cyril
similarly stayed out of sight at the organ, supporting
Andrew Maries, one of the programmes' regular
conductors, but the singing owed everything to those
Saturday morning choir practices. It was typical of Cyril
not to seek the limelight, and typical of Goudhurst also
that there were no heroics in the programme, simply
beautiful singing and the stories of a village united.

Another of the village's distinguished musical
residents living in Goudhurst during my time there had
been Vernon Coombs, a fine organist living in retirement
and the last surviving member of a club that you could
only join if you had been a German prisoner of war in
the First World War. Vernon composed his own musical
setting of a canticle sung at morning prayer in all
Anglican churches since the Reformation: every time the
choir sang the 'Benedictus' in Goudhurst, it seemed to
be telling the village's own story.

'Blessed be the Lord God of Israel: for he hath
    visited and redeemed his people;
And hath raised up a mighty salvation for us: in
    the house of his servant David;
As he spake by the mouth of his holy Prophets:
    which have been since the world began;
That we should be saved from our enemies; and
    from the hands of all that hate us;
To perform the mercy promised to our
forefathers: and to remember his holy covenant;
To perform the oath which he sware to our
    forefather Abraham: that he would give us;
That we being delivered out of the hands of our
    enemies: might serve him without fear;
In holiness and righteousness before him: all the
    days of our life.'

'Benedictus' (Luke 1:68) from Morning Prayer
in the Book of Common Prayer

29

LONDON

St Paul's: The Grandest of All!

'**W**hen I enter St Paul's, I feel how great man is, but when I enter Westminster Abbey I feel how small man is.'

G.F. Bodley, Victorian architect

The journey ends in London with a visit to the two great churches without which, Great Britain would arguably not be so great: the East Minster of St Paul and the West Minster of St Peter.

Of course, no two churches would ever claim to be rivals, especially when they are both among the most visited attractions within the United Kingdom: St Paul's Cathedral, setting for so many great national occasions, and the Royal Church, Westminster Abbey, where – ever since William the Conqueror's Coronation on Christmas Day 1066 – all but two of Britain's monarchs have been crowned. But although two of the most famous and favourite churches in the nation are just a couple of miles apart, they are very different in character.

The Cathedral Church of St Paul, London

Just as the Mappa Mundi, the earliest map of the world, places Jerusalem and the crucifixion of Jesus Christ at its centre, the sixteenth-century mapmaker, Sebastian Munster, ensured that the eye would be drawn to St Paul's Cathedral by making it larger than every other building, and putting it at the centre of his map of London.

'Here is what I know, do you know better?' asked Munster, a Franciscan monk from Germany, whose pictorial woodcut maps have helped us to see the medieval world. My own copy

of his map, published in a book of 1598, was coloured, and the artist chose to give St Paul's a blue roof to add to its importance. With a magnifier, many nearby features of London life more than 400 years ago can be spotted, such as Paul's Cross, around which the first protestant reformers would have gathered and sung psalms.

One hundred years later, St Paul's Cathedral was a shadow of its former glory. The spire shown on Munster's map had already been destroyed by lightning when the medieval cathedral was destroyed in the Great Fire of London on 3 September 1666, a conflagration made worse through wooden scaffolding shoring up the building. Lead melted from the roof and the cathedral's great bells fell to the ground.

It was not unexpected by Christopher Wren. The great architect had spent much of his early career arguing that St Paul's needed not so much repairing as replacing. Yet in meeting after meeting, no one could agree on what was to be done, or who was to pay for it.

In 1666, the whole City of London was forced to rise again from the ashes, but it wasn't until 1675 that King Charles II approved the design for a new cathedral, one that had been laid out before him by Sir Christopher Wren, scientist, astronomer, mathematician and architect. At the centre of the new cathedral would be an enormous dome, which would be visible even from the king's home, Windsor Castle, some twenty miles west, where Wren's father had been dean. Wren drew his inspiration from the dome of Hagia Sophia, once the great church of Constantinople and one of the wonders of the world, but today a famous mosque.

Sir Christopher Wren, 1632–1723 (architect of St Paul's Cathedral)

As the site of the dome was marked out and decades of building began, an extraordinary incident occurred. Wren asked an assistant to collect a stone from the old cathedral to mark out the centre of the new structure. Quite by chance, the tombstone he pulled from the ruins had the word *Resurgam* (*I Shall Arise Again*) carved on it.

It was to be in Wren's St Paul's, at evensong in May 1738, that John Wesley heard the choir sing Psalm 130. 'Out of the depths have I cried unto thee, O Lord. Lord hear my voice.' Later that same night, he took the first steps in the formation of the Methodist Church.

It was a good omen for a cathedral that would become corroded through centuries of soot and dirt, have its foundations threatened by London's tube railways and miraculously survive the bombs of the Blitz during the Second World War. No epitaph could be more appropriate for Sir Christopher Wren's grave in the Cathedral than the words, 'Reader, if you require a monument, look around you.'

'This is a special day of celebration in St Paul's,' said Dr John Moses, the recently retired dean, to the congregation one Sunday morning in May. We all tried without success to think what important date we had forgotten in the church's year. He continued, 'this is the first Sunday for more than five years when we have not had to worship surrounded by scaffolding.'

Looking around St Paul's, its stone walls newly cleaned for the twenty-first century, is to see the jewel in the crown of the nation's favourite churches, designed in the days of candlelight. The gilding, paintings and frescoes around the dome, completed only a century ago but long hidden in the gloom, now glow magnificently, lit by invisible, energy-efficient lighting, which has created a paradise for any TV camera director let loose in the building.

Visitors in the nineteenth century had a less pleasant welcome. All services were held in the choir area and a huge screen, on which the organ was placed, blocked off the high altar from the nave. The nave windows lacked glass and the whole structure became first grubby and then black with dirt. In 1870, Mr Gladstone, the prime minister, described the cathedral as 'unfinished and unseemly'. Sometimes the temperature was below freezing during worship and it took fifteen years, from 1812 to 1827, for the redoubtable Maria Hackett to win her fight to improve life for the boys of the choir.

Choir men would wander in and out, and the singers had contracts that gave them the right to be paid even after their voices had failed. And for most of the congregation, the preacher was inaudible. The Revd C.A. Belli, installed in March 1819 to sing the choral services, still held his post as precentor when he died aged ninety-four in 1886. One of his colleagues attended to his duties so infrequently that returning after an absence lasting years, a verger refused him entry to his stall.

Today the precentor is Canon Lucy Winkett, one of the first women priests in the Church of England to hold such a senior post. Her first days at St Paul's were chronicled movingly, albeit (for Lucy) extremely painfully, in a BBC2 documentary. As a woman, Lucy has acted as a natural pioneer within the cathedral's male-dominated world, but also follows the great tradition of her predecessors like Canon Sydney Smith and Dean Gregory, who in the nineteenth century struggled to transform the worship and make St Paul's more hospitable to the stranger. And yet Lucy has not only survived but thrived in such an environment. But perhaps not surprisingly, the place where she is happiest is within the deep recess of her canon's stall in the choir. Here, unseen, she can add her voice to the daily cathedral worship.

There are now 200 paid staff at St Paul's, including eight clergy, four organists, eighteen lay clerks (the men of the choir, some of whom also sing in other world-famous choirs) and forty treble choristers. There are twenty-eight regular services every week – some, like said matins, attract a congregation of only a handful, while others may be attended by hundreds, even thousands, especially at particular times of national celebration or crisis. Lucy calls evensong the liturgical rock in the cathedral's busy life:

The symbol of hope in 1940

'The institution comes to rest and worships God.'

I arrive at dusk for evensong. On the site where Christians have worshipped since 604, the men of the choir are singing a plainsong psalm. The sound seems far away and ethereal, coming from tiny distant figures in the choir stalls made in the seventeenth century by Grinling Gibbons, 'master carver in wood' to the crown, but dwarfed by richly-decorated arches. About a hundred people are sitting in the seats under the dome, with yet another hundred scattered down the nave. Every evening at evensong in England's cathedrals, the curious tourists and worn-out passers-by mingle with more regular worshippers; Lucy corrects me by saying, 'not a tourist nor a worshipper, but a person. And I trust the instinct that brings each person to church.'

But then the experience changes. Leading the music and prayer, the voice of Lucy Winkett, herself invisible in the heavenly masque in the choir, now comes across distinctly and intimately through the sound system. In contrast to the ethereal sounds of the choir, the lessons are read as if we were sitting at home listening to a friend. Then the choir sings words sung every night at evensong. No longer distant, after the versicle prayer, 'Give peace in our time, O Lord', they respond fiercely: 'Because there is none other that fighteth for us, but only thou, O God.'

It feels as if the struggle to save mankind is taking place here now, in front of our eyes. But the precentor of St Paul's makes clear in a sermon that if we are here to find a God who is 'a fierce king, a God whom we need to be powerful, and who will punish all the people we don't like, then we are bound hand and foot by our own illusion'.

The Lord Mayor of the City of London rides down Ludgate Hill in 1963

'Whether what you say in the pulpit is profound or ridiculous, you know that like a boomerang, it will come back to hit you six seconds later,' Lucy tells me when I stop to speak to her after evensong, referring to the unique reverberation and echo of Wren's cathedral. The risk of sounding ridiculous when you want to be profound is one tension that St Paul's has

Canon Lucy Winkett, precentor of St Paul's Cathedral

always accepted, for this is a living space which the nation fills with its joys and sadness, a space where the nation wishes to be welcomed, to fill not only every nook and cranny for the funerals of its heroes such as Lord Nelson or Sir Winston Churchill but also for services remembering ordinary people, such as the victims of the Tsunami disaster and of the London terrorist bombing in 2005. BBC cameras have normally broadcast such services so that not just the nation, but all people around the world can be present too.

The verses of the hymn by Cecil Spring-Rice, 'I vow to thee, my country', voted number seventeen in the *Songs of Praise* Top Twenty Favourite Hymns, expresses the two sides of nationhood like St Paul's Cathedral itself. Contributing to this special *Songs of Praise*, on the meaning of hymns, Lucy Winkett says, 'It is about our love for the country in which we live; it is also about our spiritual journey, searching for the kingdom of God.'

*'And there's another country
I've heard of long ago,
Most dear to them that love her,
Most great to them who know.
We may not count her armies,
We may not see her King,
Her fortress is a broken heart
Her pride is suffering;
But soul by soul and silently
Her shining bounds increase
Her ways are ways of quietness
And all her paths are peace.'*

30

LONDON

Westminster Abbey: A Royal Peculiar

'*There let the pealing organ blow,
To the full voic'd choir below,
In Service high and anthems clear,
As may with sweetness, through mine ear,
Dissolve me into ecstasies,
And bring all heav'n before mine eyes.*'

*John Milton describing Westminster Abbey
in his poem 'Il Penseroso'*

Westminster Abbey has been described as 'the most complex church on Earth'. In this one surprisingly small ancient building, if we knew where to look and understood what we were looking for, with time on our hands (perhaps a year or two!) we might come to understand the history of the whole world. I would choose the abbey as my 'luxury' on *Desert Island Discs*.

It is a place of history, with its floor of ancient flagstones and tombstones, a sacred space playing a unique role, where all but two kings and queens of England, and later of Great Britain, have come to be crowned. And it is a place of shared national memory, for buried here, alongside our royalty, poets and famous men, are the remains of an ordinary young man – the Unknown Soldier, representing the millions that died in the First World War.

The church that Edward the Confessor founded almost 1,000 years ago for all his people, is known as a 'Royal Peculiar' because it is still, personally, supervised by the reigning monarch, and yet open to us all. On 2 June 1953, BBC television cameras were allowed in for the first time to broadcast around the world the coronation of Queen Elizabeth II. Since then, television cameras have returned for many state occasions, including the funeral service for Diana, Princess of Wales.

Songs of Praise has come at least twice from the abbey, notably in 2001, following the 9/11 tragedy when both Muslims and Christians took part.

The Abbey Church of St Peter and St Paul, Westminster

For those of us who like history in pictures, the Bayeux Tapestry is a good place to begin the history of Westminster Abbey. This priceless strip of cloth, now on display in Normandy, not only depicts the Norman invasion of Britain and the Battle of Hastings, but towards its end shows William the Conqueror being crowned King of England in King Edward the Confessor's Benedictine abbey. The hand of God points down from heaven to the building which was begun in 1045.

The Acclamation after the crowning of Queen Elizabeth II in Westminster Abbey

Detail of the Bayeux Tapestry

In the thirteenth century, Henry III began to reconstruct the church that had become the shrine of Edward the Confessor, once king and then a saint. The nave was built over the next two centuries in a mixture of English and French Gothic styles. Early in the sixteenth century, Henry VII commissioned the royal burial chapel to be built behind the high altar, a mixture of Gothic and Italian Renaissance. It was called 'miraculum orbis', a wonder of the world. Here in ornate splendour lies Queen Elizabeth I and her sister Queen Mary, buried together opposite Mary, Queen of Scots. And it is here that archaeologists have recently discovered Edward the Confessor's own tomb.

Later in the sixteenth century, the Reformation heralded a more austere period within the abbey's history, and it was here that the famous Westminster Confession of the Presbyterian Church was agreed. Plundered by Thomas Cromwell and its last abbot, Islip and his monks, ejected when Henry VIII dissolved the monasteries, the abbey church was closed for much of 1540 and again for almost a year from the summer of 1559.

It was during the eighteenth century when building recommenced. The twin towers on the west front were added by Nicholas Hawksmoor and in 1713 Christopher Wren drew up plans for a tower and a steeple to be built over the crossing. This work was never carried out, but the architect's model still exists in the abbey, and a painting by Canaletto shows what it would have looked like.

Recently, a small but significant addition was the filling of ten empty niches above the great west door with the figures of twentieth-century martyrs, carved in French limestone. These fifteenth-century niches had never been filled so, like St Paul's, Westminster Abbey can claim to have been finally completed in modern times.

I first arrived at Westminster Abbey in the summer of 1970, a refugee from St Paul's Cathedral. It was here where the well-meaning Dean, Martin Sullivan, had delivered a sermon in which he had told everyone in his cathedral to 'go away. Go back to your own churches.' But in those days, I did not have a church to go back to. And yet new to the job of directing 'live' TV programmes every Sunday evening, I needed time on Sunday morning with, as Dame Thora Hird used to say, 'him upstairs'. So I was quickly recruited to an experience that I shared with crowds from all over the world, coming to the abbey for choral matins from the *Book of Common Prayer*.

One thing was certain. With its world-famous choir, no one in the abbey would try to recruit me to sing – a terrifying memory of childhood church for a non-singer. In fact, I don't think anyone even said 'good morning' to me. But for me, this was just what I needed, and being allowed in was welcome enough.

I usually arrived just in time to be held back by the stewards in their morning coats as the choir and clergy processed into the quire. It was my first close-up experience of Anglican ceremonial. The clergy, dressed in full fig, practised 'eyes under control', meaning that with their eyes open they looked at nothing and no one, gliding effortlessly onwards as if on ecclesiastical roller skates. I grew particularly fond of two exceptions to this studied grandeur.

Right at the back, came the then dean, Dr Eric Abbott, of aristocratic bearing and the expression of a man given to much smiling. Because of illness, he found gliding impossible, but he coped nobly with long processions, carefully led by the small but austere figure of the dean's verger, Algernon Greaves. People would literally scatter as this formidable duo

Eric Symes Abbott 1906–1983; dean of Westminster 1959–1974

emerged from the vestry, apparently steering an unstoppable course right through the middle of them, for Mr Greaves had poor eyesight and led the way largely by memory and instinct. From 1953 to 1975, he was in charge of a team of twelve, and was the last holder of the ancient office of butler to the dean. He was a kindly man with an acerbic wit and a fund of stories about the abbey. In 1977, as the queen celebrated her Silver Jubilee, he made a rare appearance in a radio interview, recalling Her Majesty's coronation. What was he doing at the moment when the Queen was crowned, asked a reverential journalist.

'Oh,' he said. 'I recall that I was enjoying a glass of Guinness down below.'

Sunday by Sunday, I returned to the south transept to wait for one particular moment, when the choir sang the last lines of the *Te Deum* – 'O Lord, in Thee have I trusted, let me never be confounded'. I would always look up at the huge rose window in the north transept opposite, trying to catch the eyes of the stained-glass apostles and prophets, praying they would help me through my evening ordeal in Lime Grove Studios.

Looking back now, I can see that the smiling dean and his clergy were quiet revolutionaries in their own way. Every Sunday, some of Britain's greatest preachers delivered carefully-crafted sermons to passing strangers. Even though we might never be seen in the abbey again, instead of being scolded or 'sent back to our churches', we were offered the gift of faith. Underneath the ethereal sound of the choir, the profound thoughts of the speakers emerged in a quiet, low-key style. But slowly, they began to sink in and I realized that I couldn't use religion as a private 'holy fix'.

I suppose when I began going to the abbey, I was firmly in the category of people that the BBC described in a survey as 'of vague faith'. I learned that I must be ready to own and argue my faith in the cynical TV world where I would spend the rest of my working life. One preacher in particular, Canon Max Warren, often spoke about what it meant to be a Christian. 'May God save us all from allowing anyone for whom we are responsible to get away with being "very religious". For then, they and you and I are missing the heart of religion: the personal knowledge of the love of God.'

Canon Warren had been General Secretary of the Church Missionary Society, and Colin Morris, a fellow missionary in Africa for the Methodist Church, described him as 'the greatest missionary thinker of his time, and a far-sighted Anglican. He always looked for the good in people; in his way, he was a saint.'

Recently, I returned to Westminster Abbey to revisit a small chapel, hidden right in its heart. St Faith's chapel, just behind the south transept, was once my place of last resort, a place that was quiet and still when the abbey was thronged with visitors. When my mother was dying, I had found this secret space very comforting but since her death, I had never been back, and thirty years on could not even clearly remember where it was.

It was quiet but not silent; the light was low, but it was not gloomy. The bleak ceiling lights and most of the Victorian chairs where I used to sit had gone, so I sat on the medieval tiled floor in front of the altar. Above it is a rare thirteenth-century wall painting of King Henry III by 'Master William, the King's beloved painter', who has included himself in it. This monk-like figure looks to his

monarch, a man of prayer, and somehow makes the chapel as welcoming as it is holy. I felt that I had come home when I realized that one of the memorials on the wall was for one of the familiar faces from my regular Sunday mornings. Inscribed under the name of Christopher Hildyard, Canon and Sacrist, who died in 1973, is his epitaph. 'An eye for beauty, a heart for friendship, a tongue for wit.'

An epitaph? Or the manifesto for the Christian life, a manifesto shared with Max Warren, Eric Abbott, his verger and butler, and countless people down the ages that have helped make Westminster Abbey a favourite church, not just of the nation but of the world? I now realize that I had not needed to look up to the rose window in the north transept to find the saints who helped set me on the road to producing *Songs of Praise*.

A Prayer

A prayer for every church and for all of us who
enter them, first used in the fifteenth century at the
consecration of York Minster.

'Lord God, grant that
thine eyes may be open
upon this house by day
and by night. Be pleased
to admit all that come to
adore Thee in this place,
and graciously to receive
them, and then,
O Lord, to hear and
to protect them
Amen.'

Glossary

Alb: A white linen garment reaching from neck to ankle worn by the ministers at communion or mass. Derived from the tunic worn in the Greek and Roman world.

Anglo-Saxon: A style of architecture used from the end of the sixth century until the middle of the eleventh century.

Apse: Vaulted semi circular end of a chancel.

Baldacchino: A canopy supported on pillars or columns over the altar.

Byzantine: A style of architecture developed in the east of the Roman Empire. Made use of round arches, domes, and mosaics. Revived in the nineteenth century for church building.

Chancel: The east end of a church where the altar is found and separated from the **nave** in the medieval church, often by a screen or lattice work called a 'cancellis'.

Chantry: A chapel usually built in medieval times, where the soul of the donor is prayed for.

Choir: The part of a church where the services are sung by the choir.

Classical: A style of architecture drawing on Greek or Roman designs.

Clerestory: An upper story in the **nave** in which windows are usually inserted.

Cope: A semi circular cloak worn at special services by priests. Derived from a Roman garment.

Corinthian: In architecture, the most elegant Grecian-styled column, having a bell-shaped capital decorated with leaves.

Crossing: A part of a church often under a central tower where the **choir** and **nave** intersect with **transepts**.

Decorated English: A style of architecture used in the fourteenth century.

Early English: A style of architecture used in the thirteenth century.

Easter Sepulchre: A table tomb, often in a recess of the **chancel**, used to depict the tomb of Christ.

Font: Receptacle for the water used in a baptism. Usually made of stone but sometimes of lead. Correctly located near the south door of a church or at the west end of the **nave**.

Gargoyle: A water spout to drain water off the roof, usually ending in the mouth of a man or beast.

Gothic: Describes a medieval style of architecture in which pointed arches are used.

Gothic Revival: The use of the principles of Gothic art applied to new materials and building techniques (*see* **Neo-Gothic**).

Minster: The church of a monastery.

Misericord: The support to a choir stall, often decorated with carved figures, which is turned up to help the clergy rest in a standing position during long services.

Narthex: Enclosed porch between a main door and the church itself.

Nave: The main body of a church, thought of in medieval times as similar to a ship to carry the congregation.

Neo-Gothic: A modern form of the principals of **Gothic** architecture applied with new technology and building materials. The predominate style of architecture used in the nineteenth century church.

Norman: A style of architecture used from the middle of the eleventh century to the end of the twelfth century. Arches are usually semi circular in shape.

Pediment: The triangular-shaped low gable surmounting the portico of a building, in the Grecian style of architecture.

Perpendicular: A style of architecture used in the fifteenth and early sixteenth centuries.

Precentor: The priest responsible in a cathedral for the direction and leading of choral services.

Quire: An older spelling of 'choir' used in the *Book of Common Prayer* in the Church of England.

Renaissance: A style of architecture describing the revival of classical art in the sixteenth century.

Reredos: Structure in stone or wood behind the altar, often decorated or carved with biblical images.

Rood Screen: A screen of wood or stone dividing the **choir** and **chancel** from the **nave**. A crucifix surmounted the screen and singers often performed here in the medieval church.

Sanctuary: The part of the **chancel** immediately surrounding the altar.

Sedilia: On the north side of the **chancel** of the medieval church, three seats were provided for the priest.

Stall: Ornate seats for clergy either in wood or stone, sometimes under a canopy.

Stoup: A small recess containing water near the door of a church. Traditionally visitors dip their hands in this water and make the sign of the cross on their foreheads as they arrive and depart.

Succentor: The **precentor**'s deputy in a cathedral concerned with choral services.

Thurible: A metal vessel for the ceremonial burning of incense. Usually suspended on chains so that it can swung.

Tracery: Stone ribs usually at the top of a church window into which stained glass is inserted.

Transept: Many churches are built in the form of a cross. The transepts are the short arms at the intersection of the **chancel** and the **nave**.

Triforum: A passage on top of the nave arches, usually on both sides of the church just under the **clerestory** windows (ideal for hiding TV lighting for the **nave** in *Songs of Praise*).

Vestry: A room attached to a church in which the clergy dress and prepare for services.

Acknowledgments

Every effort has been made to trace and acknowledge copyright holders of all the quotations and photographs included. We apologize for any errors or omissions that may remain, and would ask those concerned to contact the publishers, who will ensure that full acknowledgment is made in any reprint

Text acknowledgments

p. 9 Extract from 'Northland' © Colin Gibson. Used with permission.

p. 38 Prayer of Invocation from *Celebrate God's Presence* by Roger Harington published by United Church House Publishing 2000. Used with permission of Roger Harington.

p. 47 Extract from the song 'When the Music Fades' by Matt Redman. Copyright © 1997 Kingsway Music. Adm. by Worshiptogether.com songs, excl. UK and Europe, adm. by kingswaysongs.com, tym@kingsway.co.uk. Used with permission.

p. 57 Extract from 'Glory be to Thee O God of Life' from *Celtic Prayers* by Avery Brooke from the Collection of Alexander Carmichael. Used with permission.

p. 76 Extract from 'Longing for Light, We Wait in Darkness' by Bernadette Farrell. Used with permission.

p. 87 Extract from 'Song from Severn and Somme/War's Embers' by Ivor Gurney © Ivor Gurney. Permission granted by Carcanet Press 1987. Used with permission.

p. 91 Extract from 'Shine Jesus Shine' by Graham Kendrick (1987). Make Way Music. www.grahamkendrick.co.uk. Used with permission.

p. 100 Extract copyright from 'Summoned by Bells' by John Betjeman ©, The Estate of John Betjeman, published by John Murray (Publishers) Ltd. Used with permission.

p. 106 Extract from 'Beauty for Brokenness' by Graham Kendrick (1993). Make Way Music. www.grahamkendrick.co.uk. Used with permission.

p. 114 Extract from The *Book of Common Prayer*, the rights in which are vested in the Crown, are reproduced by permission for the Crown's Patentee, Cambridge University Press. Used with permission.

p. 117 Scripture quotation taken from the Authorized Version of the Bible (The King James Bible), the rights in which are vested in the Crown, are reproduced by permission of the Crown's Patentee, Cambridge University Press.

Picture acknowledgments

All images are © Andrew Barr unless indicated otherwise below:

Cover image and pp. 22, 23 © Robin Lee.

pp. 8, 23, 43, 88, 115 © National Portrait Gallery, London.

pp. 11, 68, 116, 118, 121, 122, 123, 124 © Getty Images.

p. 21 © F Noel. The original image is held at Hull University Archives, reference number DLB/2/86.

pp. 21, 90 © Pictures of Britain.

pp. 26, 27, 28 © Simon Knott.

p. 28 © John Everington.

p. 33 © Alamy Ltd.

pp. 40, 41, 42 © Durham Cathedral Picture Library.

p. 51 provided by Russell Darling.

p. 57 © David McLarty.

p. 74 © Malcolm Couzens.

p. 82 © Alexander Turnbull Library, National Library of New Zealand, Wellington, New Zealand.

p. 92 © The Francis Frith Collection, www.francisfrith.com.

p. 93 © Wiltshire County Council.

p. 101 © Jeremy Ley.

p. 110 © The Royal Pavilion, Libraries and Museums, Brighton and Hove.

pp. 112, 113 © Michael Bennett.

pp. 119 © St Paul's Cathedral.

pp. 122 © Westminster Abbey.